KIDS, CAMELS & CAIRO

Published by Create Space Independent Publishing

ISBN 978-1-517027-810

Printed in the United States of America

This is a work of nonfiction

TABLE OF CONTENTS

For Betty, who traveled all the way to Cairo, Egypt

and

for Sue, who would have loved to!

"Trust in Allah, but tie your camel."

~Arabic Proverb

1

HERE WE GO AGAIN

"You want to move to another COUNTRY?!" I gaped at Dan who was in the middle of cleaning leaves and dead rodents out of our backyard pool, a job he detested. "What are you talking about?!" I was suddenly concerned he was having a midlife crisis.

"Why not? We always talked about going abroad again. I'm ready to leave the school politics and cold Wisconsin winters behind. I want to live in a hot, sunny climate again, work at a school where I can enjoy being an educator, and travel on the weekends. Let's just do it!"

"Really?" I asked him incredulously. "Just leave our jobs, sell our house, and pack our bags? Just like that?!"

I was concerned that it was just another one of my husband's whims and afraid to get my hopes up until he convinced me that he was dead serious. After giving the idea more consideration, I had to agree that it felt like the right thing to do-our jobs were unsatisfying, the house we bought six years ago was a money drain, and our son would soon be off to college. Nothing was standing in our way.

✴

It wouldn't be our first time to go overseas. In June 2001, we returned to the U.S. after living abroad for ten adventurous years. During those years, we moved to four separate countries and taught in four different schools. With our one-year-old daughter, Ali, and two-year-old son, Ian, in tow, we moved first to Guam, in the middle of the Pacific Ocean, where we taught the children of the local islanders. That was also the year we survived hurricane Yuri, which swept across the small island. We next ventured to Singapore, where Dan and I taught at an international school. Ian and Ali spent their days learning to speak Mandarin while attending a local daycare center.

Ghana, West Africa, was our third overseas home. Ian and Ali attended the American school where Dan and I taught children from all across the world. During one of our school vacations, we traveled to a game park in South Africa where the four of us sat in the relative safety of an open-air jeep while a hungry pride of lions watched our every move. Five years after we left Ghana our family moved across the Atlantic Ocean to Guadalajara,

Mexico. Ian and Ali entered their surly middle school years and took classes to become certified divers, swimming alongside dolphins and humpback whales.

After Mexico, we returned to the U.S. and threw ourselves into reverse culture shock. We got reacquainted with family and friends, found jobs, bought a house, and settled into a typical American lifestyle. Ian and Ali grasped everything American as they entered their high school years, made new friends, passed their drivers' tests, and played on the basketball teams. Dan and I accompanied the other parents and cheered aloud at games, chaperoned school dances, and watched our children get through high school relatively unscathed.

The move abroad was a time of transition for all of us. While Dan and I made preparations to leave Wisconsin, Ian graduated from high school and started preparing for his first year of college. Ali accompanied us to Cairo where she completed her final year of high school at an international school. Despite feeling safe and secure in our small Wisconsin town with her close group of friends always around her, Ali felt ready for the new adventure. As parents, we still felt somewhat guilty at uprooting her and moving her to a foreign and unfamiliar environment. However, she was a good sport and went along with the plan. It was also our family's first experience living so far away from one another and we would no longer be travelling together as the "fearless four." Our fears and doubts were the only things standing in the way of making it all happen.

Our lives were about to be turned upside down and the decision to venture overseas once more was not one we made lightly. Dan and I spent many sleepless nights discussing it--were we doing the right thing for our family? Would Ian be okay without us nearby? Will Ali be okay spending her senior year in a new school, without knowing anyone? There were moments in our conversations when the move seemed too overwhelming and we went round and round discussing and arguing about it. But we always came back to our original idea of wanting to make it work.

While we packed up our household, we remembered all too well what we missed about the overseas life--the extensive travel, living with different cultures, and visiting famous worldly sites-was just a part of it. During our previous years, we also enjoyed the extra perks of tax free salaries, furnished housing, moving allowances, and complimentary plane trips back to the U.S. Those perks made working abroad a fruitful, unique, and exciting lifestyle for all overseas teachers and administrators. We were excited to have it all again.

This time around, armed with newly obtained Master's degrees and three years of administrative experience, Dan and I applied for roles as school principals. We registered for a well-known overseas recruiting fair and in February 2007, flew to Boston to take part in interviews. The fair was held at the Cambridge Hyatt Hotel over a four-day period, and attended by two-hundred-fifty American and international school representatives. Teachers and administrators from all over the world descended upon the fair with hopes of landing their dream job.

Prior to the hiring fair, I had set my sights on working at a school in Egypt. Egypt seemed exotic, and I was determined to visit the Pyramids of Giza and ride a camel one day. There was a school in Cairo that was looking to hire an elementary and high school assistant principal, the perfect jobs for us. Dan and I wanted them, but after hearing from the school that they wouldn't be attending the fair, we looked elsewhere.

We arrived in Cambridge on a cold and dreary Friday in March. After arriving at our hotel and changing clothes, Dan and I joined the other educators for an informational session. I sat in the spacious room alongside experienced teachers and principals of all ages. As I looked around I tried not to feel intimidated by their worldliness. After the thirty-minute pep talk, we got up and walked en masse into another large conference room. School directors and superintendents attired in conventional business wear, with the occasional Indian sari and African head wrap on display, sat behind tables waiting to greet potential candidates. Large spaces behind each table were decorated with oversized posters displaying school names along with their vacancies. Dan and I sidled up to a few tables to inquire about principal openings and to chat up the directors, hoping to make some contacts. We scheduled a few interviews for the next morning and went back to our hotel room, hoping the next day would bring success.

Our first interview was at 9:00 a.m., and I woke before the alarm went off, excited about what lay ahead. After I donned my one and only navy blue tailored suit, I checked myself in the mirror, and collected my briefcase. Dan gave me a quick good luck kiss and we left the room together. With resumes in hand, we joined the throngs of smart-looking teachers and administrators already beginning their hunt for the perfect school and the perfect job.

I took a few deep breaths in the elevator as we ascended the fifth floor. Dan knocked twice and the door opened to two gray-haired men in their sixties who invited us in. It felt a little odd at first to be in their hotel room, almost like we were being interviewed in their bedroom, but after we sat down and they introduced themselves and asked us a few questions, it began to feel more like a normal meeting. The men were friendly and spent most of the time telling us about their small school in Vietnam and that they were looking to hire a husband and wife team to oversee it. I smiled inward thinking to myself *'We could definitely do that! I would love to go to Vietnam!'*

The thirty-minute meeting was casual and felt more like a friendly chat. When they suddenly offered us the jobs, we could barely hide our excitement. Their offers came as such a surprise that we nearly accepted them on the spot, however, we asked for some time to think them over. As we stood up and shook hands all around, Dan asked to sign a Letter of Intent, or something official, that assured us we really had the job offers.

"No need to worry," one of the gray men said. "Our handshake is our word and our guarantee that we would like you to work for us." We left the hotel suite empty-handed and a little stunned at what had just occurred.

"We WERE offered the jobs, right?" Dan asked me as we entered the elevator.

"I think so. We shook hands on it." I replied.

"But I don't feel right not having something in writing. What if they decide they want someone else, or what if something happens and they don't need us? Didn't they also say there was a chance they could send us somewhere other than Vietnam if they needed us at another school? Who knows what we would be doing or where we would end up?" Dan responded in an agitated voice.

Despite not having received a formal contract, I still felt happy about being hired so quickly and convinced Dan to cancel the rest of our interviews. Instead, we hit the shops in Cambridge. We ended up at a Macy's store where we bought Ali an ivory lace dress for her prom, which would be coming up soon.

After our shopping expedition we took a taxi back to the hotel and dropped off our purchases. We immediately went to check our mailboxes where school directors left messages for prospective candidates. I found mine quickly and dug into it finding a message from the school in Egypt that I had contacted earlier. The message said they were now at the fair and wanted to interview us. After reading the note, I turned to talk to Dan. At that very same time Mr. Ahmed from Egypt walked up to us and asked in an accented voice, "Are you the Dobbe's?"

"Yes!" we nearly shouted at him, while reaching at the same time to shake his hand. Mr. Ahmed then asked if we would be available to meet. "Of course!" we said and scheduled an appointment for the very next morning. At that moment, neither Dan, nor I, gave a second's thought to the job offers we had with the school in Vietnam.

The interview with Mr. Ahmed was scheduled a few hours before we were to leave for the airport. I woke that morning feeling nervous, and at the same time, sick with the flu. I was miserable and just wanted to curl up on top of the hotel bed and sleep for a week. My eyes were red, my throat was sore and scratchy, and my voice came out all raspy. It hurt to talk even a little, but I forced myself to muster up enough energy to get through the interview, scratchy voice and all.

We packed our bags and pulled them along as we left our room. We pulled them into the elevator and got off on Mr. Ahmed's floor. Dan and I found his room number and knocked. He invited us into the small room and motioned for us to bring in our luggage. I giggled with embarrassment as we spent a few awkward minutes banging into each other's ankles and knees while pushing and jostling our large suitcases through the narrow door and into the tiny foyer. Mr. Ahmed invited us to sit down next to a large window that overlooked Boston's frozen Charles River. A middle-aged Muslim woman, dressed in a long, gray cloak-like garment that covered her entire body, sat in a chair directly across from us. She wore thick glasses and her pudgy hands and round face was the only body parts not covered by a *hijab (*head covering). She had a friendly smile and introduced herself as Ms. Marwa, the director of the school.

After chatting for close to an hour, we were once again stunned, when Mr. Ahmed suddenly offered us jobs. Dan and I told him we'd love to go to Egypt, and upon hearing our acceptance, Ms. Marwa jumped up from her chair and frantically began searching for two contracts. While we waited, Mr. Ahmed, Dan, and I silently gazed out the large bay window at the ice-covered river. It was too quiet and I racked my brain to think of something to say.

"Have you ever gone ice fishing, Mr. Ahmed?" I asked knowing quite well that he hadn't.

"Oh, no!" he replied with a chuckle. "I've only seen it done on the American cartoons my children watch on television." We chortled together and I pictured in my mind an animated figure sitting on top of an upside down pail on the cold, thick ice holding a spindly stick stuck into a round, frozen hole.

After Ms. Marwa located the contracts, she handed us each a copy to sign. However, before we put pen to paper, she insisted on reading the school dress code to us so that we both understood the conservative way of dressing that was appropriate for an Islamic school. Dan had no problem wearing a shirt and a tie every day of the week, but for just a second or two, I mourned my own wardrobe of cute open-toed sandals, colorful sleeveless tops, and sexy mini-dresses that would inevitably be outlawed. I hesitated for a second or two, but then quickly agreed it wouldn't be a problem for me, either. The four of us stood up and shook hands. Dan and I walked to the door and retrieved our luggage. During the course of our brisk goodbyes we managed with only a little upheaval to lug our suitcases back out the hotel door and into the hushed and carpeted hallway.

Immediately after the door closed, I shot Dan a wide-eyed look of confusion. Without so much as a glance in my direction, he held up one hand as though he was directing traffic, and stopped me from saying anything until we were safely inside the elevator. After the doors shut and the elevator lurched downward, I could wait no longer.

"Dan, what are we going to do? We signed a contract with Mr. Ahmed, and gave a verbal agreement to the guys from Vietnam. We have jobs in two countries!" I stared at him baffled.

The elevator doors opened and without answering or even glancing in my direction, he steered us out onto the main floor. With our luggage trailing behind us, we found a small alcove with deep plush chairs and sank down onto them. School officials, administrators, and teachers rushed past as we bent our heads together talking quietly.

"I don't know, Jill." Dan mumbled, covering his face with his hands. Something about that first interview didn't sit right with me. I felt the offer from Egypt was more professional and the school sounded a whole lot better."

"Okay...I know! Let's call Ali and ask her where she'd rather live, Vietnam or Egypt?" I announced. Ali knew we were at the recruiting fair and since she would be joining us overseas, we needed to include her in our decision. Dan pulled out his cellphone and she answered on the third ring. Before she had a chance to finish saying hello, Dan interrupted, "Hey honey, we're still at the hiring fair, but need to ask you a very important question. We've had two offers...one from a school in Vietnam and one in Egypt. Mom and I aren't sure which offers to accept. Where do you think you'd rather live, Egypt or Vietnam? What's your choice? We have to know right now."

"Ah, wh-what are you talking about?" Ali asked half asleep.

"Just hear us out. The drawback to Vietnam is you would have to take all your senior classes online because there is no high school. It might also be difficult for you to make any friends your own age."

"Well...Egypt then, I guess," though her uncertainty came across loud and clear.

"Well, I guess that's it then! We are going to Egypt! Thanks honey. See you soon. Bye." Dan hung up and put his cellphone back into his pants pocket. We didn't intend to leave the final decision up to Ali, but calling and talking with her reconfirmed that we wanted the jobs in Egypt more. As much as I thought Vietnam would be great, Egypt was the better choice for our family, and the place I'd originally wanted to travel to.

Soon after the phone call with Ali we ran into one of the men from the school in Vietnam. We informed him of our predicament and after a lengthy explanation and our sincerest apologies explained to him we would not be accepting the job offers. A dour expression crossed his face and he abruptly turned and walked away. We got up, grabbed our luggage, and left the hotel. Riding the shuttle bus to the airport, minor feelings of guilt about saying no to the jobs in Vietnam settled over me, however, it didn't take long for the euphoria of moving to Egypt to take over.

"We're going to Cairo, Egypt!" Dan said as he looked at me with a big smile on his face.

"I'm finally going to ride a camel!" I grinned back.

On the flight back to Wisconsin we got carried away talking about what life would be like in Cairo. We couldn't wait to get back and share the news with Ian and Ali.

Upon returning home and finishing out the school year, we also informed our colleagues that we had accepted positions at an international school in Egypt, and would be resigning.

"Egypt...like in the Middle East?" they uttered with a look of disbelief on their faces. As our announcement sunk in, we were suddenly faced with multiple questions from our friends. "How long will you be there? Is it safe? Will you have to cover your hair?" Our families were also not too thrilled, but we reminded them they could visit us any time they wanted. The reactions we received from family and friends were a vivid reminder that Wisconsinites weren't big travelers outside the U.S., and traveling to the Middle East was especially unheard of.

Our list of things to accomplish was endless and selling our house was a top priority. Dan was stressed and worried about selling it quick and after calling several realtors, put out 'for sale' signs in our front yard. He went so far as to call friends to see if anyone was in the market to buy a house. We also had several rooms of furniture and instead of selling it all at a garage sale, we bought a condo on a lake and moved it all in. The condo turned out to be a good thing for our family since we wanted it to be our home during the summers and also a place for Ian to come to when he was on his school vacations.

Also, during this time, Ian and Ali completed the school year and we gave Ian a graduation party. He applied and was accepted to a college that also recruited him for the basketball team. In the course of unearthing our passports, and blowing the dust off of them, I realized they had expired three months prior. Dan quickly sent away for new ones hoping they'd be returned in time for us to obtain our visas. It was countdown time and only months before our flight to Cairo.

On the first of June, Dan and I anxiously awaited to hear from the school. We made several phone calls and sent dozens of emails, but the school business office was on summer break and no one got back to us. We felt completely on our own as our flight date loomed closer. Dan, ever the worrier, was at his wit's end and got more upset and tense with each passing day.

A week before we were to fly out our passports arrived in the mail. There was no time to send away for the visas so we decided to drive to the

Egyptian Consulate in Chicago and apply for them in person. The four hour trip got us to the Consulate's office around noon. We found the room, walked in, and immediately explained our dilemma to the desk clerk. While appearing unfazed, she put four applications in front of Dan and told him to fill them out. We also got Ian a visa since we knew he would be visiting us during his break from college. When the paperwork was finished, we left and prayed our visas would be ready the next day. We booked a hotel room and spent the night waiting.

At 10:00 a.m. the next morning, we set off for the Consulate again. Walking along Chicago's Miracle Mile, the heel of my right shoe broke off leaving me to limp along the five long blocks. I was in a state of despair, sure that it was a bad omen and a sign that our visas wouldn't be ready after all.

But *Allah* smiled upon us.

We walked through the door of the Consulate and the clerk who remembered us from the day before, stood up and began shuffling through her stacks of paperwork. I held my breath until each visa was firmly attached to our passports. The minute the clerk handed them over to Dan, he gave a loud whoop that surprised us all, especially the frowning and cheerless clerk. I walked out the door of the

Consulate's office with a smile on my face at the exciting news that I would soon be flying to Cairo, Egypt.

Cairo

2

SALAAM ALAIKUM (PEACE BE UPON YOU)

I peered out the window as the pilot announced a rare sighting of the Giza Pyramids below. Passengers craned their necks and strained against their seatbelts to catch a glimpse of the famous structures. It had been twelve hours since we left Chicago and we were just about to land at the Cairo International Airport in Egypt.

When our plane touched down on the tarmac, I sighed with relief that we finally made it. However, it all turned to dismay the minute I entered the noisy, packed airport terminal. The assault on my senses unnerved me as bursts of loud and rapid-fire Arabic pierced the air. Egyptians and foreigners sprinted past in all directions forcing me to move out of the way. With veiled curiosity, I stared at the dark bearded men in pristine white *gallibayas* (floor length tunics) as they led burka-clad women and brown-eyed children through the terminal. The smell of cigarettes and stale sweat lingered in the dense air and I attempted to breathe in as little of it as possible. Culture shock from my first-ever visit to the Middle East hit me smack in the face.

As soon as the three of us found our luggage and dragged it off the conveyor belts, we piled it onto rolling carts and pushed them toward the main exit. Egyptian men stood clustered together holding onto placards that listed the names of passengers. We stopped to look for ours just as a dark bearded man dressed in western shirt and pants called out, "Mr. and Mrs. Dobbe?" Mr. Ahmed, from the recruiting fair appeared before us with his hand held out in welcome. Thankful to see his familiar face again after so many months, we walked with him out of the airport and toward his parked car.

I stepped into the thick Cairo heat and sweat promptly trickled down the backs of my legs. It was now July, one of the hottest months in Egypt, and I couldn't wait to change out of my jeans into something cooler. I climbed onto the backseat alongside Ali and placed my large carry-on bag on the floor. We sat together in wearied silence relishing in the cool air conditioning that wafted over us. I stared out the car window at the sights thinking it all looked so foreign. Every road sign was written in Arabic and while my eyes swept over the mysterious lines and loops, I knew for a fact I'd never master the strange language.

Dan chatted with Mr. Ahmed while he drove us through the city. Halfway there he made a quick stop at a petrol station and Dan innocently asked if there were any self-service stations in Cairo like in U.S. cities. At his question, Mr. Ahmed laughed heartily and replied, "Oh no, Egyptians would just fill up their cars and leave very quickly!" Dan laughed along with him and my mental image of Egyptian drivers filling up their gas tanks and running away as quickly as possible, made me chuckle, too. Mr. Ahmed continued driving along busy streets finally stopping in front of a tall concrete apartment building in Maadi, an upscale residential area south of Cairo, crowded with tall buildings that housed Egyptians and foreign expats. We learned later there was a lack of space in Cairo and most Egyptians ended up living in tall apartment buildings.

Anxious to see our home for the next two years, we lugged our suitcases into the building. After squeezing together into the small ancient elevator Mr. Ahmed pressed the button to go up, but the elevator didn't budge. We stared at the door for several seconds until Dan remarked, "It must be broken." Hauling our luggage back out, we dragged it all up five narrow flights of stairs to the apartment. Finding the building supervisor lurking nearby, I stood in front of the door and waited patiently for him to find the correct key. Finally finding it, he swung the door open and motioned for us to walk inside. We stepped into the dark room and my hopes of living in luxury instantly vanished. I entered the gloomy dining area which was dominated by a long wooden table and six heavy chairs. The attached living room, with its gaudy and ornate furniture, was just as dismal and bleak looking. No sunlight was visible in either of the two rooms as thick, brown draperies obscured the windows. The apartment wasn't at all what I hoped for and I didn't even bother to look at the kitchen or the two bedrooms. The place was depressing and I hated it.

Mr. Ahmed noticed my disappointment and informed us he knew of another vacant apartment nearby. I insisted we take a look even though I was ready to drop from the jetlag taking over my body. We left our luggage locked up in the apartment and returned to the elevator, which was now miraculously working. Mr. Ahmed drove us the short distance to another gray cement building and we walked up the crumbling cement steps into a lobby adorned with dirt streaked walls and peeling paint. A large dusty mirror adorned one of the walls and the filthy floor tiles looked like they had never seen a mop.

Another building supervisor met us at the door of the first floor apartment and showed us in. The building supervisors, or *bawabs,* were located in every apartment building and it was their job to take care of the maintenance and assist the tenants. I followed him into the living room and immediately noticed the modern aqua blue couch and two matching yellow and blue floral chairs, which stood out like beacons of sunshine in the otherwise drab room. The apartment included a dining room, two small bedrooms, a tiny kitchen with a refrigerator and stove half the size of the U.S. models I was used to, and one bathroom that crammed in a toilet, shower, washing machine, and clothes dryer. The few windows inside the apartment looked out onto garbage strewn alleys and the cement walls of other buildings. Although not at all luxurious, the bright living room furniture immediately caught my attention and became the deciding factor for me. The entire apartment was small and still a little dark for my taste, but it seemed much cozier than the first place.

"What do you think of this one?" Dan asked under his breath.

I whispered, "Well, if we only have two apartments to choose from, then this is the one I want."

"Okay, I guess I'll go back and get our luggage then." Dan sighed audibly and left with Mr. Ahmed. Upon his arrival at the first building, he woke the supervisor who again scrambled to unlock the apartment. When the sleepy-eyed man spied the heavy suitcases still sitting inside the room, he disappeared around a corner never to be seen again.

Ali and I stayed behind to search the rooms and check out our new home. We dug around happily finding bedding, dishes, pots, pans, an iron and ironing board, even a small T.V., which only showed programs in Arabic. Dan returned an hour later exhausted and drenched in sweat. He dumped all six suitcases onto the middle of the living room floor then collapsed onto the couch. With barely enough energy to speak, he relayed to us how he had to carry each fifty-pound suitcase down five flights of stairs because once again, the elevator had stopped working.

We spent our first full day in Cairo unpacking and settling in. We needed to buy food to fill the cupboards and the small, narrow refrigerator, so the next morning we ventured into our neighborhood to find a store. The street in front of our building was quiet and empty of traffic so the three of us drifted down the middle of it turning the corner onto a narrow tree-lined sidewalk. We walked single file stepping over upended concrete slabs that rose and fell erratically. I treaded cautiously making sure I didn't sprain an ankle or fall on my face, something I am prone to do on even the flattest surfaces. Together we strolled past rundown apartment buildings where cars parked bumper to bumper alongside the curbs. Tall trees with wide green leaves covered in layers of dust gave off cool shade, a welcome relief from the already blinding morning sun. Dogs skulked near piles of garbage and stray cats darted in and out of darkened doorways. Out on the busy roads, horns blew endlessly, scooters whizzed by, and black and white taxis congregated on nearby street corners belching out their toxic fumes.

The busy streets of Maadi were noisy and garbage strewn and after a while our leisurely walk turned into a fast-paced strut to find an open grocery store. Four long blocks from our apartment, we came upon one. Bins filled with a variety of fruits and vegetables perched outside the shop, while inside shelves overflowed with packaged and canned foods, baked goods, breads, and meats. I was elated to see a few typical American items also scattered throughout the store and after checking on expiration dates, we stocked up on Corn Flakes, tuna, milk, bread, coffee for Dan, and Diet Cokes for me. I also reminded myself to buy plenty of bottled water as we were warned many times not to drink from the tap. Lugging our bags home, I was glad that Dan had a good sense of direction since without him leading the way I would have never found my way back to the apartment. Every street looked the same.

Saturday morning came all too early. Jolted awake by the garbled prayers of an Imam blaring over a loudspeaker, I groaned to Dan, "Are we going to hear this every morning, and so early?"

"I guess so," Dan said. "I think it sounds kind of nice, and we'll never need an alarm clock, that's for sure."

I moaned and pulled the blanket over my head.

Waking up later feeling a little more rested, I was eager to do more exploring. I yearned to see some of Cairo outside our Maadi neighborhood, so we left the apartment and Dan flagged down another taxi driver. This one spoke English and agreed to show us a few of the interesting sites of

Cairo. He drove us past mosques, a few historical sites, and the old part of the city. It wanted to see more, but after driving around for two hours in the hot sun with no air conditioning, or even a breeze, as only one of the windows rolled down, our enthusiasm waned and we all had enough. Sweaty and hot from the baking heat inside the taxi, we asked the driver to take us back to our apartment. The rest of the day was spent cooling off under our one and only A/C unit turned to its highest level.

✺

The work week in Cairo begins on Sunday and runs through Thursday, with Friday being the day for worship. On that first Sunday we set off early to begin our first day of school. Ali's classes didn't start for another week, so she stayed alone at the apartment content to spend her last days of freedom lounging in her pajamas. Dan and I said goodbye to her and hailed a ride in one of the black and white ubiquitous Cairene taxis, our main mode of transportation from now on. The driver drove us to New Cairo, a wealthy area forty-five minutes from Maadi and dropped us off in front of a modern looking school building. I followed him inside and all eyes immediately drifted toward us as we walked up to the receptionist desk. A young, slim woman in a purple headscarf greeted us and I gave her our names and asked to see Ms. Marwa. While we waited I turned from the desk and peered at the modern furniture and expensive glass tables topped with vases full of dried flowers. It looked nothing at all like the musty school buildings in Wisconsin.

When Ms. Marwa opened her door she seemed shocked to see us. "Hello, welcome!"

"Come in," she said, looking taken aback as she motioned for us to enter her office. "How was your flight?"

Teachers and other administrators sat around on the couches that lined her large office. As we entered, they stood up and introduced themselves. We chatted together for a few minutes when suddenly out of the blue Ms. Marwa surprised us.

"School won't be starting for another week, so you don't have to come to work until then," she informed us.

"Oh, really?" Dan asked glancing over at me. "You mean we still have a week off?"

"Yes," she said, looking somewhat embarrassed. It was our first hint that a lack of communication existed in the school.

Surprised and completely caught off guard, we didn't stick around. Instead, we said a quick goodbye to everyone and hurried off. Back out on the street, Dan waved over our same taxi driver. We crawled into the backseat and told him to take us back to Maadi.

"Do you believe it?" Dan said. "We still have a week off! Get ready for a trip to the Red Sea."

We got back quickly and made hotel and flight reservations to Sharm-el-Sheikh, the popular resort on the Red Sea also known for its excellent diving. One of the many perks of working overseas was the opportunity to travel during the down times, and we were getting the chance to go off sooner than we had even expected. Whooping with excitement, the taxi drove us back to our apartment. Upon our arrival we jumped out and ran in the house, anxious to tell Ali the good news and start packing.

The flight from Cairo to Sharm el-Sheikh was brief, only an hour. Upon our descent, the view of the coastline was so spectacular I thought Dan was about to jump out of the plane. I held onto his arm and assured him the amazing coral reef and exotic fish would still be there when we landed. We hired a taxi at the airport to take us to our hotel. On the way there we drove past the modern one-story building where Egypt holds economic summits with leaders from all around the world. Hard to miss, a kaleidoscope of brilliant flags stands outside the building affecting a blaze of color against the beige sand.

We arrived at the resort and checked into our room which had an amazing view of the tranquil sea. Dan and Ali wasted no time putting on their swimsuits and grabbing snorkeling gear. Out on the powdery sand I went straight to the lines of beach chairs choosing one near the water, where I planned to spend my days basking in the sun. I lounged on my chair relaxed and carefree listening to the many foreign languages that were spoken around me. Behind my sunglasses, I watched European tourists of all shapes and sizes strut across the sand in skimpy speedos and scant bikinis. With no American in sight, the beach seemed overrun with Russians guzzling their vodka while tanning in the fiery sun.

"We made it!" I thought as I looked out onto the sea catching another quick glimpse of Dan's beet red and sunburnt back before he dove back under the water. *"This is the life!"*

I wasn't a big swimmer and usually more than happy to just sit and gaze out at the water, but Dan raved about the snorkeling so much that I let him talk me into trying it. Feeling a little nervous the first time out, I took a deep breath, placed the goggles over my nose and eyes, and lurched from the dock into the dark blue sea. After a lot of thrashing and attempts to stay afloat, I soon relaxed and let myself bob along. Blue, red, and yellow fish skittered below me while I swam over intricate fan and brain coral. Hypnotized by the amazing variety of sea life, I no longer worried that I was in water over my head. Later on, Dan and Ali regaled each other with the amazingly colored species they encountered--lion fish, parrot fish, huge stingrays, even sea turtles. I couldn't name half of the sea animals I saw, but still felt it was one of the best experiences I ever had; I was forever hooked on snorkeling.

"I don't ever want to leave this resort!" I told Dan as the three of us ate dinner and watched the sun slowly set.

"I love it here!" Ali announced. "So glad we could come here before school started."

"This is definitely the life! I can't wait until we tell Ian about it. I know he will want to visit," Dan stated while he stacked his many empty lobster shells onto the side of his plate.

Our impromptu vacation of sun, sand, and turquoise blue sea was a magical and memorable time for the three of us. We kicked off the school year in style.

Red Sea

3

IT HAS TO GET BETTER

Tanned and rested, we returned to Cairo ready to start work at the international school. That Monday morning as I got ready to meet the teaching staff for the first time, I took great care in choosing the proper outfit. I remembered all too well Ms. Marwa reading the school dress code to me at the recruiting fair where we were hired. From what I learned women, more than men, were held to strict standards. It was clearly spelled out that no tight or low cut clothing should ever be worn, skirts and dresses had to be ankle length, and sleeves were to be worn at all times. I understood all too well that my naked arms, legs, ankles, and toes must never see the light of a school day.

That morning I abandoned half of my wardrobe because it was either too short, too form fitting, or too flashy. I tossed pieces of clothing across our crowded bedroom and made my final choice of a dark, shapeless skirt and paired it with a long-sleeved white blouse. The blouse had a high, chin-scraping neckline and was loose enough to conceal the fact that I had breasts underneath. The only shoes that matched my conventional and tasteless outfit were a pair of black, unflattering, loafers that I'd thrown in my suitcase at the very last minute. Those shoes would become a main part of my daily outfit as women were prohibited from wearing any open-toed sandals or high-heeled shoes, due to the belief that the sounds of clicking heels on floors drew attention and distracted the male teachers. I knew it would be some time before I'd ever get to wear my strappy sandals which I carted along with me from the U.S. My gorgeous sandals would now be relegated to the back of my tiny bedroom closet where they would undoubtedly gather a layer of desert dust.

As I surveyed my modest outfit in the mirror hanging on our bedroom wall, I cringed knowing I would have to get used to dressing in this fuddy-duddy manner for the next two years. Dan, on the other hand, was happy to see me all covered up. He had already noticed that Egyptian men loved to stare at foreign women, and didn't like it.

Properly attired and ready to face the day, we joined the local and foreign teachers on the school van, which was to be our daily transportation to and from school. After the forty-five minute ride, the driver parked in the lot adjacent to the school and we walked up to the main building. Upon entering, I was nearly blinded by the shiny gray marble that covered the walls and floors. It practically shimmered and was so different from the scuffed and chipped tiles of the public schools in the U.S. I learned quickly that the impeccable sheen was the result of the continuous daily mopping by the blue maids. Easy to spot in the school with their identical blue hijab (hence, their nickname), I watched their heads bob up and down as they busily mopped the floors already at 7:00 a.m.

Ms. Marwa, looking much happier to see us this time, greeted us at the entrance and led us down one of the shiny hallways to her corner office. While Dan walked alongside her, I lagged behind juggling a stack of school materials that were about to tumble out of my arms. Just before we neared her office, I spotted an empty table and veered over to plunk everything down. Oblivious to the blue maid mopping nearby, I walked straight into a puddle of water and before I knew it, was flat on my backside with books and papers scattered all around me. Ms. Marwa, upon hearing the commotion, ran out of her office and marched straight over to the blue maid admonishing her for not displaying the yellow *Caution! Wet Floor!* sign which sat idly in a corner.

I sat up and instantly noticed that my long conservative skirt had flown up around my waist exposing my not-so-conservative red lace underpants (there was nothing in the school dress code that said I couldn't wear them!) Mortified that Ms. Marwa had gotten the full view, I pulled my skirt down as fast as I could. Bemused, Dan walked over to me shaking his head. "I heard the noise and had a feeling it was you. Are you okay?" He stuck out his hand to help me up. I grasped it and flinched from the sharp pain that swiftly shot up my leg. I twisted my ankle during the fall and it was now starting to turn black and blue.

After that fall, whenever I came near a wet floor, my pulse quickened and my body went rigid with fear. I slinked past the blue maids as they held their mops and stared at me. It was no secret to any of us why I showed dismay. At least I gave them a few minutes of entertainment in what must have been a pretty dull and tedious job.

Dan held my hand and I hobbled along next to him as we made our way to the morning faculty meeting. We entered a large meeting room already abuzz with teachers and administrators. Minutes after we found our seats, Ms. Marwa walked over to the microphone and waited for everyone to quiet down. Just as she began to speak, a harsh screech burst out of the speakers causing her to jump and teachers to cover their ears. The shrill sound was followed by a bothersome echo that ricocheted off the room's bare walls. Ms. Marwa carried on even though it was difficult to understand anything she said.

The staff sat riveted and I did my best to focus, however, I couldn't keep my eyes from drifting across the room. I looked over at the teachers and was surprised to see that many of the women wore the *hijab*, headscarves that covered their heads and necks, but left their faces open. They wore their headscarves in a variety of prints and styles and wrapped them tightly around their hair. The scarves were colorful and added character and style to their otherwise plain attire. Some of the teachers in attendance also wore *chadors* or *abayas*, long, unflattering coverings that enveloped their entire bodies from head to toe, while others wore Western jeans and nothing covering their hair.

Ms. Marwa did not wear a headscarf, but was dressed in a flowing black garment that left only her face and fingers exposed. Under her loose sleeves she wore black stretchy tights called 'armies' that covered her wrists to her elbows. It was the same getup she wore when she interviewed us in Cambridge, and during the years I worked with her, I never once saw her wear anything other than a black, gray, brown, or beige garment. I thought she must have had the most boring closet ever.

The male teachers, Egyptian and foreign, wore typical western-style clothing of shirt, tie, and loose pants to school. Only on special occasions or when visiting the mosques, did Egyptian men wear their traditional gallibayas.

Before I realized it, the meeting ended and I shifted my attention back to Ms. Marwa. She ended by wishing the staff a good school year and the teachers got up and left. I said a quick goodbye to Dan who sauntered toward his office in the high school. With my ankle now throbbing and swelling to twice its size, I limped up the three flights of stairs to my own office. A small room located right next to the stairs, it held a gray metal desk, filing cabinet, and two chairs. There was one large window which looked out over the high school and a spacious green lawn. In the corner of my office was a bathroom I had all to myself. I felt like a queen and was thrilled to no longer have to use the smelly student bathrooms where I had to bend down to wash my hands or view myself in the mirror. Enthusiastic to start decorating, I filled the walls with colorful student artwork I found sitting in a corner. The artwork seemed to be just what the room needed to look and feel cheery. With my office set up I felt ready to greet the students and begin the school year.

✱

Three days later, on another sunny morning, Dan and I left our apartment and waited at the corner of our street for the school van. After we climbed on we were surprised to see students, along with teachers, filling up the seats. We greeted everyone and before we even sat down, the van took off into the busy traffic.

Our ride that morning seemed almost too short and we got to school quickly. I stepped off the van and walked toward the elementary area. Excited dark-haired Egyptian children of all sizes and ages chased back and forth while waiting for the first bell to ring. I stepped with caution into the unruly fray and navigated through the mobs of eager elementary students, praying I would make it to the building without any mishaps.

With my arms holding tight to a box of school materials, I forged ahead toward the main doors of the elementary building. Just as I reached out to grab the door handle, a curly-haired boy came out of nowhere and ran smack into me knocking me down. It was several seconds before I even realized what had happened. Tears sprang from my eyes as oblivious students jumped over and around my inert body. My tears were not only from the pain I was feeling (which was now spreading across my entire backside), but more the result of getting knocked off my feet by a scrawny ten-year-old. I looked at the lanky boy and waited for some kind of apology, or help even. Instead, he gave me a lopsided grin and dashed off to join his friends in their game of tag, or more like, hit-and-run. Angry and hurt, I forced myself to stand up. It was the first day of school and already the second time I lay flat on the ground. No one came to help, or even ask if I was okay. Once again I swallowed my pride, gathered up my box of materials, and limped into the school.

The first day of the school term had begun.

4

RIDING ON CAMELS

Great Sphinx

Days off from school occurred often and for a variety of reasons. The major Christian and Muslim holidays of Ramadan, Christmas, and Easter were celebrated with several weeks off. We were also given time off because of political demonstrations, bad traffic, and polluted air. We even had a day off when President Mubarak's grandson died unexpectedly.

Two weeks into the school year, we had our first three-day weekend and Dan, Ali, and I were anxious to finally visit the 5,000-year-old Giza Pyramids. On a clear, smog-free morning in mid-August we left our apartment and flagged down a taxi. Dan stuck his hand out and gave the upside down wave used by all Egyptians as a signal to stop. Within seconds a car screeched to a halt in front of us. We slid onto the cracked vinyl seats and were instantly engulfed in the pulsating Arabic music that blared from the radio. Grunting a quick hello and barely looking at us, the driver sped down the Corniche Road that ran alongside the Nile River. I stared out the window as we raced past gray apartment buildings with brightly painted shutters and doors. Lines of wet laundry were strung across the high, flat roofs, while numerous satellite dishes sprouted like mushrooms from even the most dilapidated structures.

On that clear, sunny morning I spotted the pyramids off in the distance and pointed toward them to show Ali. Jutting upward into the blue sky the very sight of them took my breath away. When we entered Giza City, the residential area that bordered the pyramids, I knew our taxi was getting close. The dark blue *nazar* (evil eye) swung recklessly from the rear view mirror as our taxi bumped along the pockmarked main road swerving away from pedestrians, animals, and vehicles. Camels clopped along the street while donkeys and bulls pulled overloaded carts. Motorcyclists weaved between the cars and modern, air-conditioned tourist buses careened past. A polluted canal filled with plastic bags, empty bottles, rotten food, even dead goats, dogs, and horses, divided the wide road in half. I turned away and looked in the opposite direction so I wouldn't have to see the deplorable sight.

After the forty-five minute drive from Cairo, the taxi driver let us off onto a dirt road near a camel stable. We jumped out of the doors and a bearded man wearing a long gallibaya and a wide smile on his face walked toward us. My husband, Dan, met him halfway and explained that we wanted to rent three camels and a guide to take us into the desert. The smile never left the Egyptian man's face and I was sure he was already counting the money he knew he would make from us.

Very much the naïve tourists, we had no idea what the going rates for camels were. Mr. Camel Boss probably thought he hit the jackpot when Dan made a few futile attempts at bargaining. After agreeing on a fee I watched the two of them shake hands hoping we didn't get ripped off too badly. Three rented camels adorned with bright red tassels waited nearby, and we hesitantly sauntered toward them. Dan chose his camel and quickly hopped on. With a boost up from the guide, I straddled Layla, my camel, and together we lumbered single file down the rutted path toward the desert. Egyptian camels are trained to walk in a line behind the other camels. They can also get very testy if they are put in the wrong order, but luckily for us, we didn't witness any of their "tempers."

From the time we accepted jobs in Egypt, I looked forward to this moment. My dream of riding a camel was really happening and I sat proudly on top of Layla, bouncing along. She didn't seem to mind me on her back, but she did sideswipe a few cars and a couple of people that got too close to her. After a few moments of enjoying the view from atop Layla, I eventually gathered up my courage to look down from where I sat. I let out a yelp the second I noticed the sheer distance from me to the ground, and from then on, my eyes stared straight ahead and I relaxed into Layla's gentle sway.

Tall and regal animals, camels have very unique personalities and whimsical facial expressions. They appear almost cute with their quirky and lackadaisical attitudes, but quickly lose their charm when they flash their thirty-four, brown-stained teeth and spit, vomit, sneeze, or fling slobber around. Camels also have a mean side and are known to kick their spindly legs in all directions, making it necessary to always approach them from the sides. It's also good to know that when they cool themselves off they like to pee on their legs, and yours, if you stand too close to them. And oh, those incredible sounds they make. The guttural noises they emit when forced to sit down or stand up sound so menacing. I couldn't help but giggle every time I heard one of the camels bellow.

Feeling a bit unsteady about approaching such a large animal, I carefully moved toward Layla's side. As she lay immobile on the ground, I stepped into the stirrup and lifted my right leg up high swinging it over Layla's back. Once I proceeded to get myself upright in the saddle, I leaned way back holding on for dear life. Layla rocked her immense body back and forth while she stretched out her hind legs and prepared to stand up. The guide then told me to lean my body forward, and after a few jerky wobbles, Layla stretched out her front legs and stood to her full, towering height. Sitting on top of Layla while she attempted to stretch out her legs and stand was a little like getting tossed around on a carnival ride--jarring, unstable, and nerve-racking. With several audible gasps from me and a couple of lusty, anguished groans from Layla, she got into position and the lurching finally ceased.

As Layla sauntered along, I fantasized myself a lone female Bedouin ambling across the quiet and isolated dunes on my way to a distant Bedouin camp. However, the longer I was out there, the more I sweat and the more uncomfortable it became. The golden sun was scorching and tiny grains of sand stuck to my skin, hair, and clothing like glue. Despite the blistering heat, which radiated off the dry landscape, it was my first camel ride and I was enthralled by the enchanting experience. Our small caravan ambled along into the desert and Ali turned around to snap photos of Dan and me. Even the camels smiled and mugged for her shots.

Our guide led us straight to the pyramids to get a closer view. When he asked if we wanted to go inside, Dan never hesitated, "Are you kidding? YES!" Our camels were forced to lie back down and after a minute or two of getting jostled about they lay still and we climbed off. Like bowlegged cowboys we walked up to the rocky entrance of the Great Pyramid, the oldest and tallest of the three. I crouched underneath the small opening and followed Ali down the narrow stone steps which led into a hot and cramped alcove. It was dark and claustrophobic underground and the earthy smell of dirt and clay hung heavy in the air. The detailed hieroglyphics and colorful murals depicting bold scenes of ancient life covered the rocky inner walls. Since the walls had never been exposed to harsh sunlight, their colors were still vibrant. An elderly man stood guard beneath the pyramid and watched our every move. He was there to stop us photo happy tourists from taking pictures, but for a small *baksheesh* (bribe) of a few Egyptian pounds, he turned the other way and let us click away. Later, Dan watched our guide pay the tourist police to look the other way so that we could climb up the outside of the pyramid. It seemed everyone liked to make a little money off tourists. I couldn't help but feel a little guilty since I knew we were adding to the slow destruction of the pyramids, but it was a once in a lifetime chance and I took it.

It's hard to believe that no machinery was ever involved in the building of the pyramids. Stranger still, scientists have still not discovered the true reason behind them. Theories exist that try to answer the question of who built them, and vary from aliens, Noah of Noah's Ark, and even Satan. There are also stories that portray the reasons they were built--as tombs for pharaohs, to store grain, and as landing pads for aliens. One theory even speculates that ancient Egyptians used their own mental powers to lift up massive boulders and drop them into place.

As well as touring the three more famous pyramids, we also visited the Step Pyramid with its six steps built on each side, and the first pyramid built of stone. The Bent Pyramid is the most unusual and it changes shape halfway up. I thought the Egyptians must have had a very clever sense of humor, or they built that pyramid for practice.

Giving our camels a rest, we walked onto the sand and moseyed around the structures. Our guide continued to relay the history of the pyramids, but I only heard half of what he actually said since I was now too tired and hot to listen.

After we left the pyramids, we got back onto our camels and rode further into the desert. In the middle of nowhere a mustached Bedouin man on foot, carrying a jumble of white scarves, or head wraps, appeared in front of us. He jumped right into his sales pitch refusing to take "no, *shokrun*," (no, thank you) for an answer. In order to get rid of him, Dan broke down and bought three head wraps and for a few more Egyptian pounds, the greedy desert-dweller wrapped each of them around our heads, Bedouin style. After making his sale he bid us farewell and strode off across the sand dunes looking for more gullible tourists.

An hour later our tour ended near the Great Sphinx. Our guide brought the camels to a halt and tapped each one of their bony legs with a long, thin whip forcing them to lie down. My body lurched forward again as Layla folded her long legs and lay down for a well-deserved rest. Hot and gritty, I climbed off and patted her on the head before walking over to the massive structure with the head of a human and the body of a lion.

Ali and I wearing our head wraps while sitting on Layla

The Sphinx was carved from a single stone and Ali and I walked around the entire figure as it sat in splendor guarding the pyramids. It was fascinating to see it in person after only seeing photos in *National Geographic* magazines. Like the Giza Pyramids, it was so much more impressive in real life, but also distressing to learn that the figure was slowly crumbling due to the wind, smog, and pollution that filled Cairo's air. It was a humbling experience standing next to the noble stateliness of the Great Sphinx, which is believed to be the greatest monumental sculpture of the ancient world.

Tourists from around the world flocked to the Giza Pyramids on a daily basis. Lined up side by side in the sandy parking lot, tour buses spit out tourists, along with their black, offensive fumes. In anticipation of earning Egyptian pounds, camel guides wait for the innocent and gullible visitors to come along. The aggressive and relentless guides pounce on the tourists, begging, pleading, and stalking them until they give in from sheer exasperation.

On a later excursion when my family visited from the U.S., we waited almost an hour for my brother and sister-in-law to return to our group. They finally appeared from behind one of the pyramids, sweat-soaked and furious. They rushed toward us exclaiming that one of the persistent camel guides followed them and continually harassed them for money. He wouldn't leave them alone and when they tried to get away they got turned around and ended up in between two pyramids unable to find their way out.

Despite the greedy camel handlers, the Giza Pyramids were monumental and majestic, just what I expected.

5

A DIFFERENT KIND OF SCHOOL

The teachers who worked at our international school came from all parts of the world--U.S., Canada, England, Australia, New Zealand--but the majority of them were from Egypt. Egyptian teachers weren't always qualified to teach and were sometimes hired simply because they were practicing Muslims. It didn't take long for the foreign-hired teachers to burn out from frustration over students' disrespect, belligerent attitudes, incessant talking, and constant classroom disruptions. Socializing, more than receiving an education, was the priority of many students. There was very little parent or administrative support and some teachers got so fed up they left before the school year ended. Stories abounded of disgruntled teachers who went on the three week winter holiday and never returned. The school then scrambled to find available teachers to substitute the classes. Around five months into the school year, I also felt the discipline problems would never end and knew this wasn't what I signed up for.

Blindsided by the Islamic culture, I knew very little of the ways of life, traditions, and beliefs. I'd never met any Muslims growing up in Wisconsin and it wasn't until I moved overseas to Singapore, a melting pot of world religions, that I first encountered them. Lucky for us, our colleagues were always willing to teach us what we wanted to know.

Curious to learn the types of foods Egyptians ate, I found out that our librarian had a catering business on the side and hired her to cook for us. She made Egyptian and western food and once a week I scanned her small menu and ordered food to bring home. Her western dishes included spaghetti and mac 'n cheese, but Dan and I wanted to try Middle Eastern cuisine. She made great kebabs, kofta (ground meat mixed with spices), and *kushari* (a mixture of rice, pasta, spaghetti, lentils, and chickpeas in tomato sauce). Neither one of us was crazy about *mahshy* (vine leaves stuffed with herbs) though, which seemed to accompany a lot of the dishes, and we soon ended up with a freezer full. Just like other foreign foods, Egyptian cooking was an acquired taste and after a few weeks of eating traditional foods, we reached our limit and only ate them sparingly.

I tried to fit in with my Muslim colleagues and chatted with them in the staff lounge, assisted them in classes, and socialized outside of the school day. The first time I was invited to a colleague's home I looked forward to a real Egyptian experience. The event happened to be a get together for female guests only and was held at an apartment outside Cairo that had a picture-perfect view of the Giza Pyramids.

On the afternoon of the gathering, a taxi delivered me to the hostess' gray nondescript apartment building. I entered the dirty stairwell and hiked up several flights of stairs to the fourth floor apartment, then walked inside. Groups of teachers arrived behind me and as soon as the door shut, I watched as they threw off their burkas and unwind their elaborate headscarves. No men came anywhere near the apartment so the women were free to expose their curvaceous bodies, rouged cheeks, and shiny hair that lay softly around their shoulders. The overbearing cloaks were gone and the teachers I worked with on a regular basis looked, and even acted, ten years younger. Individual personalities burst forth as the women laughed and gossiped with one another, nibbled syrupy Egyptian sweets, and swayed their hips to loud Middle Eastern music. It was a festive gathering and for several hours the women reveled in their independence. When the party came to an end and it was time for everyone to leave, the teachers gathered up their cloaks and covered their hair again making sure every last strand was out of sight. Fully enshrouded, they swiftly left the apartment and entered the male-dominated city once again.

Dan also tried to get to know his colleagues in the high school and struck up a friendship with Yousef, one of the IT teachers. When the school computer system crashed, which happened often, Dan called on Yousef to get his up and running. One afternoon while they waited for the computer to reboot, Yousef chatted with Dan and entertained him with stories of working with the Bin Laden family in Saudi Arabia. Yousef divulged to Dan that Osama Bin Laden would drop into the workplace and shout orders willy-nilly. The office staff, even members of Bin Laden's own family, thought him crazy and ignored his ridiculous rants.

Months later another member of the IT staff was let go after allowing his students to look at porn during computer class. For safety reasons, Dan was told to personally escort the teacher out of the school doors. Local Egyptian staff members were upset, especially as the IT teacher's sister also taught at the school. Dan was not very popular with the staff for a while.

I learned that members of the Islamic Brotherhood were also employed by the school, but I never noticed anything political go on. In 2011, several years after we left Egypt, we heard about the Egyptian Revolution through news reports. During that time, Egypt's president, Hosni Mubarak, resigned from office after thirty years. He was replaced by Mohammed Morsi, a member of the Islamic Brotherhood. A year later Morsi was forced to resign and his resignation caused a great deal of political strife between the Brotherhood and the military backed government. Tourists left Cairo, embassies closed, and many Egyptians were injured and killed during the riots.

During our first year in Cairo, trouble broke out in the Gaza Strip when Israeli Defense Forces hit homes in the town of Beit Hanoun. It seemed everyone at our school had relatives or knew someone living in Gaza. Worried and concerned for their safety, the atmosphere at school was one of panic and sadness for the Palestinians. In order to show support, the school's male students started wearing the black and white checkered *keffiyehs* over their school uniforms to show support for the Palestinians against the Israeli occupation.

Listening to colleagues talk about their fears for their loved ones made me feel closer to the situation. It was my first time experiencing the aftermath of a war-like situation and I wanted to do something to help the Palestinian children. Upon learning that many of the homes, schools, and libraries were destroyed, I organized a school-wide collection of toys, clothing, shoes, and blankets among the staff, students, and parents of our school. I was amazed at how much was collected and on the last day, I packed it all into boxes and the school arranged for a truck to take it into Gaza. I was proud at what we accomplished and pleased to be able to do something worthwhile for the Palestinians. I was surprised that I didn't have more support from the school owners or administration. After the collection I never received any word that the boxes actually made it there or helped anyone in need.

Matrons, or errand girls, also worked throughout the school. They sat outside classrooms and waited for teachers to call on them to make copies, deliver messages, or walk students to the principal's office. They did not speak English, and when not running errands often sat reading their miniature-sized Qurans, huddled together in gossip, or fast asleep in their chairs. My own matron, Samia, was young and spoke some English. Her days were spent sitting at a small student desk outside my office waiting for me to send her on errands. I often found myself running up the three flights of stairs to my office. Since the floors looked identical to one another, I often bypassed my floor forgetting which one I was on. When Samia saw me she'd yell for me to stop, saving me from ending up on the roof.

A small army of security guards stood all day long by the front and back gates of the school. They wore spiffy uniforms, carried holstered guns, and wrote on clipboards that they always carried with them. The guards didn't seem to really do much other than keep track of who came and went from the school.

Arabic is the official language in Egypt, but our students and teachers spoke English, as well. When Dan and I first arrived in Cairo we hoped to learn Arabic. Dan was determined and began practicing it during the van ride to and from school.

"Won't it be great when I can surprise my high school students with the Arabic words I've learned?" he asked excitedly.

Each time we rode the van, he made sure to sit next to one of the Arabic speaking teachers. With his English-to-Arabic dictionary in hand he enlisted her help in pronouncing the difficult words. The young, shy teachers loved to help Dan and always smiled warmly as they patiently taught him to count in Arabic. However, it wasn't too long before he gave up. His days were exhausting and he found the language much too difficult. By the end of each day he just wanted to sleep and often nodded off for the entire ride home. We did however manage to learn a few basic words adding them to our small repertoire.

Women in Cairo seemed to dress in their individual ways. Most Muslim women wore hijab (headscarf). Some of them wore a long, full-bodied garment, called a *chador*. The more devout wore *niqabs* (face veils) and burkas. Some chose not to cover their hair at all and tended to wear more Western-style clothing. It was common practice for devout Muslims to begin wearing hijab around puberty, and the reasons varied from being a personal choice, advised by their father, husband, or God, or because it was the traditional way of dressing.

The government in Egypt does not dictate what women should wear. However, many Muslim women wear hijab by choice, or because of social pressure. It seemed that once a Muslim woman decided to cover her hair and body it was difficult to end the practice. We had female staff members at our school that stopped wearing hijab and suffered occasional harassment by other hijab-wearing teachers.

Many teachers wore headscarves to keep their hair and necks covered, but they seemed to have many practical purposes, as well. Women who wore headscarves spent less money on hair styling products and less time in front of the mirror. They never had to worry about bad hair days and their hijab protected them from the burning rays of the Egyptian sun, as well as freak rainstorms (even though there weren't many in Cairo). Headscarves also warmed a woman's ears during the bitter winter months where temperatures dropped and cold winds blew. I especially liked how chic Egyptian women looked in their designer headscarves, which accentuated their dark eyes and face. Fortunately for me, foreign women weren't expected to cover their hair as I would never have been able to tie my scarf in that complicated manner. It also wasn't a good look for me, no matter how many different ways I tried to wear one.

Dan was captivated by the director, Ms. Marwa's, demeanor whenever he saw her walk through the school hallways. In her long, cloak-like garment, she reminded him of Darth Vader, the fictional character from Star Wars. The only difference was she didn't emit the heavy breathing sound when she walked.

Ninja Warriors is what came to my mind every time I spotted Muslim women standing together in a group. Clothed in their long, black cloaks with only their dark eyes peering out, the shadowy women resembled the characters. I couldn't help staring at them, even though I knew it was rude; they looked so mysterious and intimidating to my sheltered Midwestern eyes. Covered all in black it was virtually impossible to read their facial expressions or even know who they were. It was also disconcerting for me to see women wearing niqabs while out driving cars. They were so thoroughly covered I didn't know how they could possibly drive safely, or even see around their blind spots. Those small rectangles just had to restrict their view and cause accidents.

We immersed ourselves in Egyptian daily life right from the beginning. Dan and I had a lot to learn about Islam and Muslims and our occasional cultural faux pas got us into trouble. Once, when Dan brushed up against a female teacher, he noticed that she moved her chair far away from him. Later, when he tapped her on the arm to ask her a question, she turned and matter-of-factly informed him that men were forbidden to touch Muslim women.

On another day while Dan was working in his office and listening to jazz on his computer, Kareem, one of the more conservative teachers, entered his office, gave him a strange look, and walked back out. Baffled, Dan couldn't understand why Kareem left so abruptly without saying a word. He learned later that it was *haram* (forbidden) for conservative Muslims to listen to music, which was also the reason there was no music department at our school. Music was among the many western influences that were forbidden by Islam, along with dancing, eating pork, homosexuality, wearing jeans, cursing, masturbating, and playing chess.

The Quran is the Islamic Holy Book that guides the lives of most Muslims. Respected for its teachings of Mohammad, every Egyptian teacher had her very own personal copy sitting on top of her desk. During breaks, they crouched over their Qurans reading and praying silently. Once, without realizing my blunder, I walked up to a teacher's desk and put my half empty can of diet coke on top of her Quran. Aghast and in a huff, she removed it, picked up her holy book, and put it in a safe spot far away from me and my infidel soda.

A well-known Hadith from the Quran states, "When one is not reading or reciting from the Quran, it should be closed and stored in a clean, respectable place. Nothing should be placed on top of it, nor should it ever be placed on the floor or in a bathroom." Another cultural faux pas I wished I had known about.

Separate staff lounges existed for males and females within our school. Each lounge had comfy chairs and couches with tables, and the requisite floor space for prayer mats. Several times during the day teachers unfolded their rugs, knelt toward Mecca, and prayed. Mecca, in Saudi Arabia, is Muhammad's birthplace, and the place where Muslim's believed Muhammad talked to God. It was believed that praying to God five times a day (known as *salat*) allows them to have a personal connection with him, remembering him throughout the day.

Whenever I visited the staff room and saw teachers praying, I lowered my voice not sure if talking out loud was considered disrespectful. But when I noticed that others kept right on conversing, I did the same. After a while, witnessing teachers bent over in prayer just became part of the school scenery.

It was a jolt to my small-town Midwestern values to learn it was culturally acceptable for cousins to marry in the Middle East. In order to keep their vast wealth within the families, arranged marriages were often set up early on. I was surprised when told the owners of our school were first cousins and that we had teachers on staff married to relatives. It was a practice that I just couldn't get my head around.

I was also blown away to discover that our Muslim staff did not believe in the Holocaust or the fact that a man walked on the moon. Those were renowned historical facts that were a part of everyone's education. When the new and immaculate high school library was completed and the librarian ordered thousands of books to fill the shelves, many had to be returned due to inappropriate subject matter considered offensive to Islam. No books were allowed in school that mentioned Jerusalem, the Holocaust, or that a man had walked on the moon.

Racism was also prevalent in Egypt. The school wouldn't hire Hindus and many Muslims overtly despised Israelis and condemned homosexuals. There were very few Blacks in Cairo other than African refugees, who were looked down upon by the general population because of their skin color and different ways of dressing.

During the time I spent in Cairo, my eyes were constantly opened to the customs, beliefs, and traditions of Islam. There was much more to the Muslim people and their way of life than was presented by the world media and I was thankful I had the opportunity to live for a time in their world.

6

I CLIMBED MT. SINAI (BARELY)

A month after school began, Muslims prepared for the holy month of Ramadan. For thirty days, from dawn until sunset, they abstained from food and drink in an effort to purify their bodies. It was my first Ramadan in a predominantly Muslim country and I didn't know what to expect.

During the long school days, our devout colleagues fasted while they continued to teach their classes. Not surprising, energy levels were low and some teachers had a hard time getting through the day. I wanted to support them and made sure whenever I had the urge to eat or drink something, I hid beneath my desk, or in the bathroom. With the hot Cairene weather and blood-sugar levels plummeting among our female staff, it was not unusual for one or more of the matrons to lapse into a dead faint during the day. Whenever one of the blue maids or matrons collapsed, the other matrons ran to her, picked her up, and scurried her away to be revived. Dan became quite concerned one day when he noticed so many fainting in the high school. He felt he couldn't just sit and do nothing, so he gallantly ran to the rescue each time he was in the vicinity of a faint woman. But after he lifted and carried off five matrons in one day, he decided to let the school doctor deal with them and called her to help instead.

When Ramadan officially began, shops and restaurants remained closed until sunset, the time that fasting ended. For us non-Muslims, it was very inconvenient. If we wanted to eat out or shop, we had to wait patiently for the sun to go down before we ventured out. At sunset, the local shops and restaurants opened and were inundated with noisy and hungry Muslims as they shopped for *iftar*, the meal eaten after sunset. Special foods were prepared and the meals were huge social events that often lasted late into the night. After not eating all day, Egyptians gorged themselves with as much food and drink as they could handle. The next morning at sunrise, the fasting commenced all over again. Many students and teachers fell asleep during classes tired from their late night feasts.

When Ramadan ended thirty days later, Muslims celebrated *Eid-ul-Fitr*, known as 'breaking the fast.' This was a special time when families bought new clothes, attended prayers at mosques, and gifted food, money, and clothing to the less fortunate. Families prepared and ate traditional foods. Any animal killed for the final *Eid* feast had to be prepared according to Islamic ways, when Allah's name was pronounced at the time of the animal's slaughter.

Following the initial thirty days of Ramadan, school let out for a week. Dan, Ali, and I decided to join several teachers in renting a van and driver for a ten-hour excursion to Nueiba Beach in the Sinai Peninsula. Prior to the trip, the European teachers requested that the American staff take a separate van. In the past, the Americans often got stopped at the border, which forced everyone to be detained for hours, and no one wanted to go through that again. However, we all stayed together in one van and never once got stopped.

I learned of an earlier trip to the Sinai when a military officer pulled over a group of teachers. He flagged down the van after noticing a teacher snapping photos of officers and military vehicles. After the driver pulled to the side of the road and stopped, the officer jumped onto the van, walked over to the photo happy teacher and confiscated his camera and the damaging photos.

On our way to the beach we drove through a major tunnel beneath the Red Sea near the Suez

Canal and emerged onto the peninsula. From there, we continued for another two hundred miles and reached Nueiba in total darkness. When we finally stopped and the van doors slid open, I grabbed my bags and headed straight to our hotel room. It was too dark to see the water or anything else around us so we went straight to bed exhausted from the long trip in the van. The next morning, with the sun high in the sky, I donned my swimsuit and headed out to float in the crystal clear water. Spread out in front of me was the Gulf of Aqaba with its white sandy beaches and remote lagoons. Further off in the distance I could see Saudi Arabia's mountains reaching into the sky, providing a dark, craggy backdrop. The quiet beach was unoccupied except for the occasional camel that strolled languidly by. After a few dips in the gulf, I lounged on the weathered pillows and threadbare carpets inside a traditional Bedouin tent that lay on the sand. I basked in the tranquil and serene setting until word got out to the neighboring Bedouins that foreigners had arrived. Soon, a small group of sun-wrinkled women descended upon us and plopped themselves down onto the sand. They unloaded their bags of cheap plastic trinkets and persistently wheedled us to buy from them. Not at all interested in their fake jewelry, I did get some great photos of their kohl-blackened eyes and wizened faces. Despite our lack of interest, they refused to leave until the owner of the hotel came out and shooed them away.

Mt. Sinai, where God gave Moses the Ten Commandments, was only a short distance from Nueiba Beach. Also nearby was St. Catherine's Monastery, the oldest inhabited monastery and home to an ancient outgrowth of the sacred burning bush. Mt. Sinai, at 2,600 feet, was a popular trek for devoted pilgrims and tourists from around the world. I didn't know much about the mountain, but our colleagues raved about the climb. They all said that the spectacular sunrise at the very top was worth the climb. Dan and Ali got caught up in the excitement, and in the end I let them talk me into climbing Mt. Sinai with them. Only later did I realize not a single person told me they would do it again, which should have tipped me off.

"You have to experience the top of the mountain at sunrise," people remarked. "It's a fantastic experience!"

Others who had climbed Mt. Sinai, cheerily exclaimed, "It's not a bad hike and you will truly regret it if you don't do it!"

I'm not a climber and never had the slightest desire to go up a mountain. I don't even like to walk up steps, but found myself getting into the spirit. I figured it'd be a nice leisurely morning hike with a glorious sunrise to top it off.

I was so wrong.

The night before the climb, I tucked myself into bed and slept a handful of hours before waking at midnight to prepare for the journey. Still half asleep, I dressed quickly stuffing my minimal climbing gear of water, flashlight, and sweatshirt into Dan's backpack. My only shoes besides flip flops were a pair of flimsy sneakers that had little, if any, support, however, they were all I had and I put them on without a second thought.

As the rest of the hotel guests slept on, I left our cozy room and walked out into the pitch black night with Ali and Dan. I squinted up at the dark sky illuminated with billions of stars and climbed into the minivan, which sat idling in front of the hotel. The driver immediately sped off taking us down dark, lonely roads eventually stopping near St. Catherine's Monastery. We gathered our backpacks, left the van, and walked silently past the closed monastery toward the base of Mt. Sinai.

Clusters of camels wearing colorful tassels around their necks huddled together. The animals grunted loudly and their handlers tried to entice us to ride up Mt. Sinai on their backs. The last time I rode a camel was in the flat desert and my body shook with fright at being up so high. I couldn't imagine sitting on one of those bouncy creatures while it clopped along the narrow paths mere inches from the edge of the mountain. *No thanks!* I thought to myself. *I'm more than willing to see this through on my own two feet.* We just started the climb when we came upon three rickety wooden huts filled with a variety of soft camel hair blankets, shawls, and ponchos. No way was I going to pass up a chance to shop, so I begged Dan and Ali to stop and wait while I ran into the first hut. I immediately purchased a velvety soft shawl and after wrapping it around my shoulders, rejoined Dan and Ali. We picked up the pace and set off again.

There were two paths up Mt. Sinai and we picked the shorter one. At the time I hoped it was the easiest path, if there was such a thing. As we walked, we passed by groups of tourists chatting in multiple languages. I couldn't help but observe that most climbers were much better equipped than me, even wearing expensive climbing boots. I looked down at my shoes and wondered if I was being a bit naïve about the difficulty of the climb. However, it was too late to turn back so I kept walking, my flashlight illuminating the way. An hour into the climb we encountered a rugged staircase that was chiseled into the rocky mountainside. Known as the "steps of penitence," the 3,750 steps were supposedly built by an Orthodox monk as his penance. *Great,* I thought to myself. *What a nice monk; helping climbers by going through all the hard work of building steps.* However, it wasn't long before the uneven and jagged staircase became torturous to climb. My feet throbbed and my knees ached. It was also about this time that I fully realized I wore the worst shoes ever.

It remained dark and cold for several more hours while I continued my slow arduous trek. The surrounding darkness made it difficult to see other climbers until I was right on their heels. Even more problematic was when the camels barreled past and forced me to stop and move over to the very edge of the path. I thought for sure one of the brutish beasts would sideswipe me and knock me clear off the mountainside. Not only was I extra careful not to fall over the side of the mountain, but I did my best to also avoid the piles of poop they left behind.

An hour into the climb, I was sick of it. We were still a long way from the top and my enthusiasm was long gone. One hour passed, then two, and each time I asked Dan if we were getting close he just shook his head, dashing any hopes I had of nearing the top. After an hour of huffing and puffing, he began to worry about me and regularly asked if I was okay. By then I was so beyond tired I could barely croak out a response. Exhausted, out of breath, and losing what little patience I had left, I brooded, *if he asks me one more time how I'm doing I will push him off this godforsaken mountain*.

Not long into the trek, Ali, and a friend sped off ahead so they wouldn't miss the sunrise. I had also hoped to witness the spectacular sight that everyone raved about, but at that moment, I couldn't have cared less. I was still nowhere near the top and we had been climbing for three-and-a-half hours already. Each time I was sure we were closer, I looked up only to see we still had a long way to go. The climb felt like a death march and just as the sky began to lighten, I gave up. I veered off the path, found a large, flat rock, and promptly plunked my butt down.

"I refuse to go any further. You go ahead and I will wait right here," I calmly announced to Dan.

"But you can't stop now, we are almost there!" he pleaded.

"Oh, YES I can, AND I will! I AM SICK OF CLIMBING THIS EFFING MOUNTAIN! I keep thinking the end is near and it NEVER COMES! I AM SICK OF IT! YOU GO!" I bristled.

"Okay, then I will stay here with you," Dan remarked as he sat down beside me.

I was convinced we were bound for divorce right there on biblical Mt. Sinai. I cried, I screamed, I begged, but he refused to go on without me no matter how many swear words I lobbed at him. While we continued to argue back and forth, four agile young men dressed in the latest mountain climbing fashions trotted by. Upon witnessing our argument, one of them turned and exclaimed excitedly, "You're almost there! You gotta' keep going!" I looked up from my rest stop and gave him a look that could have melted the rock I reclined on.

"Oh, sorry to interfere!" he said and rushed passed to catch up to his climbing buddies.

After sitting on that rock a while longer, I stood up and began the climb again. Without saying a word Dan followed close behind. He stopped once to pick up a small rock and dropped it in his pocket. He would later give 'the piece of Mt. Sinai' to his father as a keepsake.

We finished the rest of our excursion in silence. I stepped onto the very top of Mt. Sinai just as the sun peeked out in all of its glory. Cheers erupted as the yellowish glint spread across the mountain top. I cheered along with the other climbers then crawled on all fours to find an open spot to sit. With so many climbers converging on the very top it was difficult to find an area not already occupied. With wobbly legs I crab-walked over the sharp rocks and squatted on top of the sacred mountain. I sat for several minutes entranced by the breathtaking views of the surrounding red mountains. From my high perch I looked out at the majestic scenery and felt like I was on top of the world.

Near me on the very edge of the mountain top was a small cottage believed to have been built on the same rock where Moses received the ten stone tablets. Known as the Chapel of the Holy Trinity, it once held priceless artifacts, but was now closed to the public.

The experience on top of the mountain was just as amazing as everyone said it would be, that is, until I realized I had to get back down the mountain. After soaking up the last of the heavenly sunrise, I got up onto still shaky legs and made my way over toward the path. I practically skipped, so sure that going down would be easier. Things, however, didn't go quite so smoothly and in no time a line of climbers started passing me. Moments after slipping and sliding down the rocky path, I tumbled and fell down, causing multiple shrieks from the other climbers. I got right back up and carried on as I knew there was no other way to get to the bottom, and I was desperate to finally get there.

On top of Mt. Sinai

After four grueling hours of walking uphill, and then another four going downhill, I was ecstatic to step onto flat ground again. I could have jumped for joy if only my body didn't ache so much. We met up again with Ali and Millie, an elderly teacher friend, who opted to ride one of the camels up the mountain, instead. On her way back down on foot, she ended up taking a different route and got lost. After we all commiserated over the agony we had just endured (yes, it was mostly me) we walked over to St. Catherine's to get a peek at the distant cousin of the burning bush.

Our group gathered inside the building where tourists and devoted pilgrims converged on the small area creating a mass of wall-to-wall people. The bush sat in a fenced off space while mobs of tourists surrounded it. With the area so congested, none of us could even get close to it. Dan, who towered over everyone, stretched his arms and just barely touched the tips of the branches. The devotees who got close to it attached small pieces of paper that held their personal messages and prayers.

Bone-weary from my climb, I wasn't too excited about a bunch of sticks, no matter how old or sacred they were. After getting up at midnight, then climbing up and down a mountain for eight hours, I could barely stand. All I wanted to do was get in the van, drive back to the hotel, and collapse onto something soft and cushy for the rest of my vacation.

But it was not meant to be.

✱

When we signed up for the climb at the hotel, I had insisted we also book a visit to a traditional Bedouin camp (what was I thinking). I originally looked forward to the opportunity of observing Bedouins in their natural habitat. Since it was my idea to go, I mustered up the little energy I had left and crawled back into the waiting van. Before I even slid the door shut, the driver sped off onto the dirt road. In the middle of nowhere he turned onto a secluded trail filled with deep potholes. I held on to my seat, bouncing in all directions, until the driver came to a stop in the middle of the desert. I trailed behind the others and crawled out of the van. A stocky middle-aged Bedouin man wearing a long, flowing and impressively white gallibaya walked toward us. His head was swathed in a red and white keffiyeh and held in place by a black *agal*-rope, a symbol men wore to show their manhood.

"Salam Alaikum" (peace be upon you), he yelled to us as we sauntered toward him.

"*Alaikum Salam*" (and peace be upon you), we mumbled with forced enthusiasm.

Desert tribes from the past were nomadic and moved their families to different areas so that their animals could graze near water. The Bedouins we saw in the Sinai tended to stay put, relying on tourist dollars for their income. They carried cell phones and drove massive Land Rovers and fancy SUVs.

Upon entering the campsite, our host led us over to a large round open-air tent made of animal skins and hides. The small space smelled like goats and my eyes surveyed the soiled pillows, frayed woven rugs, and tattered cushions that lay on top of the hard, packed sand. Outside the tent, scrawny goats were tied to a few scraggly trees and one lone camel stood stock still staring blindly into the sunlight. Two small, grubby boys with mucus streaming from their noses stared blankly at our group. Fat, black flies buzzed around their shy, oblivious faces and clung to their moist eyeballs. It was a disturbing sight, but also one that was hard to look away from. Dan especially fixated on the boys' faces, finding it hard not to stare. He talked for days afterward about how the flies circled the boys' faces and stuck to their eyes.

Our host motioned for us to sit inside the tent while a quiet woman, whose face was as wrinkled and dark as a raisin, arrived with sweet tea in tiny glass cups. She wore a black burka and embroidered niqab decorated with gold coins that tinkled when she moved. With downcast eyes she set the refreshments in the middle of the rug. *Shokrun*, we said aloud, thanking her in Arabic. We perched together on the grimy cushions, while our host sprawled out lengthwise, like a king on his throne. I tried to make small talk, but our Bedouin host was more interested in chatting up the younger women, Ali included.

The same woman came back out to collect our tea things and returned with a vast silver platter filled with rice and pieces of boiled chicken. We inched toward the mound of rice, staring at the feast in front of us. I noticed one large serving spoon which came with the chicken and rice, but there were no other utensils. Bedouins typically eat with their fingers and it looked like we were expected to do the same. None of us was excited about eating. I wondered if it was even edible as there was nothing resembling a refrigerator nearby. After a couple of us attempted to eat a few bites, we informed our host we weren't hungry (even though we had just climbed a mountain and hadn't eaten anything since dinner the night before). The silent woman returned to the tent and retrieved the nearly full platter. No doubt, she and her children gorged themselves on the abundant meal that we paid for, but couldn't eat.

After the meal we were all more than ready to leave the campsite. Our new friend, and host, drove us in his shiny new Land Rover back to the hotel, most likely anxious to collect his hefty pay for giving the tourists a true Bedouin experience. On the way he stopped and picked up a friend who flagged him down from the side of the road. The look of utter shock on the Bedouin hitchhiker's face when he climbed into the back of the van and noticed it filled with foreign women, was priceless, and made us all laugh. He continued to joke, keeping us in stitches as he offered each of us one hundred camels to marry him.

After returning to the hotel, I stepped out of the Land Rover woozy with exhaustion. The short walk to our hotel room was pure agony. I hobbled on my bruised feet until I fell onto the bed and remained there for the rest of the afternoon and on into the next morning. We set off back to Cairo after breakfast. After the long drive back, I was more than happy to see concrete again. I had enough sand,

mountains, camels, and Bedouins for a very long
time.

7

DARN

Our school did not have a high school, so we enrolled Ali into another Egyptian/International school for her senior year. After her initial nervousness, mostly due to being one of only a few non-Egyptians, she got used to her new school.

Despite not knowing anyone and not speaking a word of Arabic, we hoped she'd make the best of it. Ali tried hard and put on a brave face for us, but the guilt was still there. There were nights when we heard her crying in her room because she missed her friends back home. It was heartbreaking and we hoped she'd make some new friends soon and life would get better.

Ali's new school was more or less across from ours. It was difficult to say just how close the two schools were since the entire area was covered with sand and the few dirt paths made it difficult to walk or drive from one school to the other. Dan did attempt the walk once, thinking it closer than it actually was, but by the time he got there, his shoes were filled with sand, his shirt was ringing wet with sweat, and his face and neck had turned an odd puce color from the blistering heat.

The school called itself an international school, but was predominately Egyptian. The students weren't very welcoming to non-Arabic speakers and cliques among the girls were already formed at young ages. We were happy when Ali got invited out socially, however, we knew that alcohol was a big part of student festivities, despite being illegal, and Dan, always overprotective, often followed her to make sure she was safe.

When Ali got to know a few of her classmates better she soon realized how different from her they actually were. Most of the girls came from very wealthy families and often went on weekend shopping trips to Paris, not at all like Ali's life. In classes, teachers often mistook her name for a male's. Pronounced differently from the popular Middle Eastern boy's name, it was still spelled the same. Ali's name and her yellow-blonde hair often made her chances of blending in difficult.

Several weeks after school began she observed how the students loved to play pranks on their harried and overworked teachers. After getting off the bus and arriving home one afternoon, she told us of an incident that occurred in her physics class.

"I walked in and all the boys (she happened to be the only girl) were standing on their chairs, shirtless, and dancing,"

"What did you do?" I asked laughing.

"I barely glanced at them and walked straight to my desk. When the teacher came in he told them to put their shirts back on and to sit down."

By that time, Ali had witnessed so many bizarre student behaviors that she wasn't even fazed. Joining the school as a senior, she also missed out on taking International Baccalaureate courses and got stuck with the less demanding subjects, which resulted in classmates who were not exactly high achievers. During that year however, she joined the yearbook staff, attended her senior classes, and put up with the juvenile antics of her classmates, all while waiting patiently for the school year to come to an end.

Dan was especially eager for Ali to have some fun in Cairo. Before moving to Egypt, she played basketball and he thought if she joined a women's team in Cairo she would be happier. He searched and found one at a local sports club and Ali joined the group of mostly college-aged Muslim girls. She was the youngest player and one of the few who didn't wear a headscarf. The players welcomed her, but only a few spoke English. The coach didn't speak any at all and it was a problem for her at times because she didn't always understand the plays, or what the coach wanted her to do. Ali came home frustrated and in tears after many games, but hung in there and never missed a practice. As a result, she made the starting lineup and was a major contributor to what was a competitive and successful basketball team in the greater Cairo area. We were very proud of her, and Dan was always at her games and practices rooting for her.

Meanwhile back in Wisconsin, Ian was now in his first year of college. He was also on a basketball team and busy with practices. We left for Cairo weeks before he began school, but he was ready to be on his own and looked forward to his future. After he moved into his dorm and received his class schedule, Ian phoned us with news that centered on how expensive his books were, how tiny his dorm was, and how bad the cafeteria food was. We talked weekly through Skype, and Dan and I were able to follow some of his basketball games over the internet. No matter what, it was still difficult to be away from him, and we missed him.

When the December break came up, the three of us flew back to Wisconsin and found ourselves shivering from the cold, while attending Ian's college games and celebrating Christmas with our families. Ali was happy to reconnect with her friends and after three frantic weeks we found ourselves back on the plane heading to Cairo.

In June, when she finished her senior year, Ali decided not to take part in the graduation ceremony since she never developed a fondness for the school or her classmates. As payback for coming to Cairo, and her graduation gift, we bought her a plane ticket to fly to Europe. Since we also felt guilty for leaving Ian behind when he started his first year at college, we also flew him to Cairo, then on to Europe. Together with their backpacks fully loaded, they flew off to Amsterdam, Brussels, and Paris. Our two globally-minded children were now adults who wanted to experience traveling on their own. Dan and I felt proud and finally, guilt-free, as we drove them to the airport and waved them off to begin their well-deserved European adventure.

❋

Typical international schools enroll students from many different countries mirroring a mini-United Nations. Our school, despite calling itself an international school, was Egyptian and Muslim. The three students in the entire school who weren't Egyptian stood out like "sore thumbs;" the pressures of not being Muslim or not speaking Arabic, eventually became too much for them and they left.

The majority of our students were born into Cairo's wealthiest families. They lived in fabulous walled-in mansions and had households run by nannies and maids. The nannies often did the main child-rearing and chauffeurs drove students to and from school in luxury family cars. A few of the school's families even had private planes that flew them to exotic locales all over the world.

The families were used to having others work for them and the parents and students often treated school employees as their personal servants. Parents were never allowed to enter the building during school hours as they were disruptive and often caused scenes. Most parents however, flocked to yearly parent-teacher conferences and turned them into major social events. Mothers wearing their long, dark cloaks also dressed in designer shoes and carried expensive Gucci, Louis Vuitton, and Chanel bags over their arms. Their bejeweled fingers were covered in four-, five- and six-carat diamonds, rubies, and emerald rings that glittered and sparkled. There was so much bling on display that during parent meetings I had to force myself to look into their faces, even though my eyes insisted on returning to the large baubles attached to their fingers. The wealth of the families was unfathomable.

The fathers of our students traveled a great deal so discipline was left mostly to the mothers. Many had little control over their sons and often left meetings in tears when confronted with their child's horrible behavior. The Egyptian kids seemed sweet and docile on the outside, with their dark features and incredibly long eyelashes that most western women would kill for, but those innocent faces were deceiving and even the foreign teachers, who were better trained in classroom management, found them difficult and unmanageable. Parents blamed teachers for "not loving their kids enough," and teachers blamed parents for a lack of discipline and structure at home.

Many of our students also had the same names. More than one Mohammed, Omar, and Abdullah resided in every classroom. The girls also had identical names making it difficult to remember who was who. If I was unsure about a boy's name I would just call him, "Mohammed," and chances were pretty good that I would be correct. I could say the same name aloud in the hallway and no less than ten boys would turn around and look at me.

Throughout the entire school up through grade twelve the boys outnumbered the girls. The boys were disrespectful to teachers and talked constantly during classes. They also got into more trouble for fighting and using bad language. Inappropriate words filtered throughout the hallways, but because I didn't understand a word of Arabic, I never knew what they said. However, I did learn quickly that calling another Muslim a "donkey" or a "dog" was a major insult and one that guaranteed revenge.

Our elementary students already had a good idea of what their futures held. They often didn't feel any need to take responsibility for their bad behavior and liked to blame it on someone else. Parents believed their sons were little "princes" who never did anything wrong. When summoned to my office they came in demanding, "What did I do?" The boys were good actors, but when confronted with their behavior they pleaded and begged for mercy. "Please, Miss Jill! I swear!" was their common response and they believed that swearing to God would get them off the hook. When I informed them they needed to change their negative behavior, they'd respond with *Insha'allah*, (if God wills it). In other words, they believed their behavior was left up to God, and they had little control over it.

During breaks, the boys loved to play soccer, the national sport. But because they were so aggressive, fights often broke out. Teachers suffered from the heat in their long garments and sat in the shade instead of supervising the boys on the field. The girls had little to do other than run around and play tag; only once did I see them play something different. I watched with curiosity once as a group of twelve stood in a circle singing and dancing. They giggled and twisted their little bodies from right to left while they clapped along to a song. It was refreshing to see them play a girly game and I couldn't help but laugh and sing along with them. However, after that one time the girls never played it again. When I asked why not one nine-year-old told me that her mother said it was haram for girls to sing and dance in public. It struck me then how early they were taught their roles to be quiet, docile, and submissive.

Classes were conducted in English, and in addition to math, science, social studies, and language arts, the students also attended Arabic and Quran classes. Each day they participated in noon prayers inside the mosque, which was located in the basement of the school. When the bell rang, elementary students bounded down the stairs, took off their shoes, and tossed them aside. They lined up at the sinks to perform *Wudu*, the traditional cleansing ritual that shows respect to God. Every student washed his head, face, hands, and feet, leaving the floor slick with puddles of water. When finished, they moved into their separate carpeted areas and got ready for prayers. In all mosques, males and females are separated. I was told that it was so boys and men did not become distracted, and were able to keep their minds on their prayers.

The girls' section of the mosque was located behind a temporary wall. A small square window opened up and carried the Imam's, or in this case, the Quran teacher's voice, through to their section. Before prayers, the girls donned their small white veils and got into their lines on the carpet while talking quietly to one another.

The boys, on the other hand, loved to race to the carpet and slide on their stocking feet, as if they just entered a skating rink. If the Quran teacher was nowhere in sight, which was often the case, the boys also used the time to wrestle and practice their acrobatic skills. It was my least favorite part of the day and I spent it trying to instill calm and order among eighty excited boys. I often checked my watch over and over as I waited for the Quran teacher to arrive. On those days, I even begged Allah to make him appear quickly.

Sometimes, being the main elementary school disciplinarian and assistant principal was a grueling and thankless job. Students and parents got angry if I gave consequences and if I didn't, teachers accused me of being too lax. I tried to instill the values of honesty and respect, but without support from parents or other school administrators, I often felt powerless, ineffective, and very much alone. Several years after I left the school, I learned that three people were eventually hired to do the exact work that I did completely on my own.

On one particular quiet morning while working in my office, I was interrupted by an irate art teacher. She stormed through the door and was followed by seven fifth grade boys. Distressed and agitated, the teacher informed me of the boys' behavior then left me to deal with them. The guilty boys stood mute before me with their eyes fixed on the floor.

It was almost lunchtime and noon prayers were about to begin. After I lectured them for a few minutes, I ended with a warning, "You darn well better pray after showing such rude behavior toward your teacher!" When I noticed their eyes momentarily get wider and a look of shock cross their faces, I felt sure I had gotten through to them this time. However, when they left my office mumbling to one another in rapid Arabic it never crossed my mind that I would be the one in trouble.

I arrived to school early the next morning and learned I had caused a major frenzy among the boys' ultra-conservative mothers. All seven of the boys had gone straight home to announce that I had insulted Islam by using the word "darn." My words were misconstrued by both the boys and their mothers as the story was relayed over and over on parent cellphone chats. It never occurred to me that my using the word "darn," a word that also meant "to mend or repair," could be taken so wrongly, nearly inciting an international incident.

Getting revenge for a wrong done to you was a basic right taught to Egyptian students. Many students used the phrase, "It is my right!" to explain away their verbal or physical bullying. Students were supported by their parents and told to fight or hit back if someone did the same to them, the complete opposite of what I tried to teach them. The mothers of those fifth grade boys got their revenge on me.

At the end of the school year, the entire staff gathered to watch a farewell video organized by the parent organization as a special thank you to teachers and staff. Everyone listened as a pleasant musical soundtrack played and photo after photo of faculty members popped up onto the screen. When photos of the administrative staff came into view, I waited to see mine. It finally showed up, but instead of placing me with the other school administrators, the parent organization, made up of the mothers of the fifth grade boys, relegated it to the very last page alongside photos of the school workers, secretaries, and matrons.

Angry and humiliated in front of all the teachers, I wanted to get up and run out of the room. Dan held onto my arm and forced me to stay put. I eventually calmed down and was glad I stayed. Soon after, my name, Dan's, and the names of other foreign staff that were leaving the school were called to the front of the room and the rest of the teachers and administration stood up, clapped, and gave us a heartfelt tribute. I will never forget how the Egyptian students and parents made me feel, but most importantly, I won't forget how supportive and understanding the expat staff was.

Dan, our taxi driver, and I sitting at an outdoor café

8

MANIC STREETS OF CAIRO

It didn't take long for the twice daily van ride to become monotonous. Dan usually fell asleep while I spent most of the ride gazing out of the windows, reading, and chatting with teachers around me. Students' heads rolled onto their chests while they nodded off into unconscious slumber. It was free transportation and I tried not to complain since taking taxis every day to school would have been too expensive.

Our school was located outside of Cairo and south of Egypt's Police Academy in the middle of a vast desert. It was built in an up and coming area called New Cairo, and despite all the new construction, miles of sand still covered the region. Large plots were bulldozed by heavy machinery that left deep tracks in the sand. Vacant, half-constructed apartment buildings and other large structures were erected as a new city started to emerge in the desert. Hundreds of dark-skinned construction workers toiled all day under the scorching sun while they climbed scaffolds, removed large rocks, and mixed up large vats of cement. Squatters, the families of the workers, lived inside the empty and stark buildings where they cooked their meals over fires and hung wet laundry on top of half-built cement walls. Their many children ran barefoot and played games on the big piles of dirt and sand that littered the area.

Drab cement structures melded with the neutral color of the sand making for a dreary landscape as far as the eye could see. Despite the long distance from the Nile, attempts were made to beautify the desolate and baked area. Green trees and pink and purple flowers popped up among the dry cacti and rocks, while large, full grown palm trees were trucked in to give the area a greener, healthier look. Our daily van rides also took us past a large shopping center and an enormous mosque, which was in the process of being built in the sandy oasis. We never got to see the completion of either one, however, as construction was halted due to the owners of the buildings running out of money to pay workers or buy more materials.

The drive to and from school took us along Cairo's Ring Road, a dangerous highway congested with vehicles and pedestrians. Horns honked and tires screeched amidst the madness. Car lanes and posted speed limits were nonexistent and vehicles whizzed by at breakneck speeds. Slow moving donkey carts and pedestrians hugged the far sides of the highway, oblivious to the Mario Andretti-like drivers that sped past them. Vehicles swerved in and out of long lines and narrowly missed pedestrians that attempted to cross the nightmarish thoroughfare. Men, women, and children ran for their lives to get to the other side of the death trap highway. Most were lucky to escape with their bodies intact, but every now and then, we'd spot a dead body lying alongside the highway.

On one particular morning, I saw the still body of a man lying face down on the road. I couldn't get him out of my mind and all day I pictured him lying there motionless. I wondered who he was and how long he'd be there before someone removed his body. Death was a big part of Egyptian life. Muslims were big believers in the afterlife. Ancient and sacred tombs and burial chambers for the pharaohs were part of Egyptian history. But when I thought about the many deaths due to fatal car accidents in Cairo it made me question how much the lives of ordinary Cairenes were valued.

Driving in the center of the city was just as challenging and dangerous. I was aware of only one traffic light in our Maadi neighborhood and we never once saw it work, assuming it was there merely for decoration. City traffic often came to a halt whenever buses picked up passengers or street vendors blocked the roads. The many narrow streets were congested with too many cars. Impatient drivers navigated around motorbikes, pedestrians, and even goats and sheep. Cars drove bumper-to-bumper and the slow traffic tested drivers' patience. Irritable men often lost their cool. They jumped out of their cars in the middle of the roads screaming and yelling profanities at one another. Much to the delight of pedestrians nearby, the drivers flailed their arms in attempts to slap one another. The commotion was usually over nothing more than a small scrape or fender bender, known to Cairenes as a "Cairo kiss."

Black and white taxis clambered along Cairene streets like swarms of jumbo-sized beetles. They scurried between cars and honked their horns continuously. The foul exhaust and constant horn blowing drove me crazy. But despite being such loud and smelly nuisances, they were still our main mode of transportation and a very cheap way to get around. On short trips around town, we either walked or took a taxi, but when we wanted to see other parts of Egypt, we rented a car and driver. Renting both was easy and a great way to see the surrounding towns and villages without worrying about getting lost or dealing with police barricades.

Many Cairenes also rode motorbikes around the city. While they zoomed in and out of the relentless traffic jams, it was typical to see an entire family perched on one small motorbike, with nary a helmet in sight. Mothers sat sidesaddle and held their babies on their laps. Fathers squeezed a child or two in between themselves and the handlebars. Since it was often their only transportation and also the quickest and cheapest way to travel together, Egyptians always found ways to make extra room on their motorbikes.

Cairo's Metro, established in 1987, was one of two subways in Africa. It was a quick form of travel and cost only one Egyptian pound (13 cents for one trip). Having taken the Metro only once, I found the cars crowded, dirty, and stifling in the heat. Women had separate cars from the men, although men sometimes forced their way on and suffered the wrath of female passengers who screamed and yelled for them to get off.

Riding in the women's only car on the Metro

Traffic issues were only one of Cairo's many problems. Overpopulation, environmental issues, and noise pollution also plagued the city. Sexual harassment--catcalls, insults, vulgar gestures--are such a huge problem that in 2013, the United Nations reported that 99 percent of Egyptian women experienced some form of harassment. For a long time shame made women reluctant to report the abuses, but today, more women are reporting them and seeking justice. I sincerely hope that harassers are brought to justice and women living throughout Egypt speak out for the respect they deserve.

I was never comfortable walking alone on Cairo's streets and rarely went out on my own. The Egyptian men loved to stare and often made annoying "ssst" sounds to get a woman's attention. I heard stories of men grabbing and groping women in broad daylight, then running away. Not sure if it was because they considered western women loose, or because they were sex-starved, but the harassment was rampant. Whenever Dan was beside me it drove him crazy to see Egyptian men gawk so blatantly. His 6'4," two-hundred-pound frame, never seemed to deter them either. He made loud and sarcastic comments at the glaring men, but since most didn't understand English they basically ignored him, and continued to stare.

Thankfully, I was never accosted while in Cairo, but I was witness to an indecent act that threw my Midwestern values for a loop. On a late afternoon power walk in a residential area with two friends, I thought I noticed a red car following us. The driver seemed to inch forward and then speed off as soon as we got closer to him. When I realized that it in fact we were being followed, I stopped dead in my tracks and screamed in shock, "That car is following us!"

The driver gained on us once more. This time as he got closer, we marched up to his window and caught him with his zipper down and his hand inside his jeans. We yelled a stream of obscenities and pounded on his car windows. The three of us made as much noise as possible until he sped off around the corner.

We laughed through the rest of our walk and hoped we didn't give the pervert a chance to finish his business.

❋

It was several years after 9/11 and Muslims were still a big part of the world news. There didn't seem to be any anti-Americanism and I felt safe, mostly due to the uniformed and gun-toting tourist police that occupied every corner of the city. Dressed in their impressive white uniforms with weapons dangling at their sides, the young officers spent most of their time gawking at women and making loud, rude comments. I never heard of any thefts or murders during the time I lived in Maadi, which surprised me since the police were not exactly hard working. When they weren't leering at women they were often sound asleep with their heads balanced precariously on the ends of their long guns.

9

OUT AND ABOUT IN CAIRO

A felucca sailing along the Nile River

Weekends and holidays from school were the best times for us to explore different areas in Cairo. We depended on the city's many taxi drivers to get us to the places we wanted to go. Taxis were easy to find, even if they weren't always in the best shape, and drivers were eager for fares. The more chatty drivers loved to tell us about Cairo and talk politics. Dan liked to get their opinions on President Mubarak and when he asked what they thought of President Bush, they replied without hesitation, 'Bush bad!'

Late one Friday afternoon, feeling tired and bored from the relentless Cairo heat, we decided to cool off with a ride on one of the feluccas, Egypt's traditional sailboats. The taxi driver dropped us off at a spot on the Corniche Road where a fleet of feluccas sat bobbing up and down on the Nile. From that spot we walked single-file down a set of concrete steps and neared a row of empty wooden feluccas gently swaying in the water. Feluccas are still used today as houseboats for poor Egyptian families and as transportation up and down the river. Tourists who want to take a leisurely trip down the Nile can also rent them out.

Ali and I followed Dan as he walked to the river edge and approached one of the boat captains about negotiating a price for an hour long trip. They settled on a price of LE 30 ($5.00 US) and shook hands. We climbed aboard and settled onto ratty cushions that lined the long wooden seats. As we set off, the felucca captain raised the large white sails that flapped in the wind. Early evenings at sunset were always the most enchanting times to be on the Nile. The calm, cool breezes pushed us along and we glimpsed Cairo's skyline and watched the scenery of the grassy banks go by. I loved floating on the calm river. It was quiet and peaceful; a nice reprieve from the constant noise and hubbub of Cairo.

Two weeks later we explored Islamic Cairo, the oldest and most historic part of the city. After arriving on the outskirts, I instantly felt as though I stepped into medieval times. A very different experience from the rest of busy Cairo, I ogled the thousand-year-old minarets, mosques, and colonial churches with their beautiful ornate and embellished architecture. I listened as the recorded and stern voices of Imams calling all Muslims to prayer drifted through the air. While strolling down the narrow and congested streets beneath the wooden-latticed balconies, I passed by mothers covered in black burkas who held tight to their children's hands, never once making eye contact. Adjacent to the ancient part of the city dirty streets, dilapidated buildings, and decaying architecture sat alongside newly-remodeled buildings which housed modern shops, cafes, and restaurants, making Cairo a hodgepodge of old and new.

The Khan el Khalili souk is a main shopping bazaar that sits inside old Cairo. Upon entering, I quickly got sucked into the noisy, bustling crowds that strolled along the narrow and winding alleyways. Amongst the seven-hundred-year old medieval arches and craft stalls, tourists and Egyptians browsed for bargains, skinny cats raced through the lanes, and fat rats scurried into the sewers. I held my breath against the odors of rotting garbage and raw sewage while I attempted to push my way through the mob. The overcrowded paths, constant shouting of vendors, and rude stares of Egyptian men turned the entire place into a madhouse. Too many bodies filled the bazaar, which made shopping an exhausting and daunting experience, not for the faint hearted. The most difficult part for me though, was trying to find my way out of the maze and back out onto the streets of Cairo.

Within the souk, stalls sold t-shirts, perfume, papyrus, silver, alabaster trinkets, and glittery belly dancing costumes. Gold and antique vendors spread out their sparkling wares in glass cases, while spice sellers displayed bins filled to the brim with aromatic and colorful seasonings. Bread delivery boys, called *agalati,* whizzed down the lanes on bicycles, ringing their bells and balancing trays of flat, round bread on their heads. Shrill shop vendors shouted and cozied up to tourists enticing them to buy, or "have a look for free!" I made sure to avert my eyes so they would leave me alone; I knew if I gave them even a brief look, or touched anything at all, they would harass me until I bought it. I found that out when I stopped to look at a knee-length black tunic with intricate black embroidery on the front. I told the vendor it was too small and as I started to walk away he shouted to his helper to run and get me a larger size. It took the helper three tries to find the right one and after causing so much trouble I felt I had to buy the tunic, whether I liked it or not. Vendors also loved to yell out to Dan asking him how many camels he wanted for Ali. They must have thought it was funny, or just something the tourists liked to hear, because they all said it. Dan ignored them, but after my own shopping sprees, threatened to swap me for a few camels.

✳

The massive Muhammad Ali Mosque sits high on a hill and overlooks the round domes and tall minarets of the Islamic part of Cairo. It is the most popular tourist site in Cairo and sits in a fortress called the Citadel which opens onto a large courtyard. On the ride to the mosque, the driver informed us it was also known as the Alabaster Mosque because alabaster was removed from the tops of the pyramids and used in its construction.

It was another sizzling hot day when we paid a visit to the famous mosque. Ali and I wore typical western clothing of short sleeved tops and Bermuda shorts. Since our clothing was considered unacceptable attire for the sanctity of the mosque, we were forced to put on drab green tent-like burkas that were made available to female tourists. We put them on over our clothes and it wasn't long before we were both sweating from the additional fabric. Removing my flip-flops, I placed them at the entrance along with the other footwear and stepped inside the large open space. I walked with bare feet onto the worn red oriental carpet that covered the entire floor. The inside walls of the mosque were covered with Egyptian marble and alabaster. Peering upward, I was dazzled by the many tiny bright lights that hung from the brilliant chandelier. A raised platform stood against one wall and was used for reciting prayers. A smattering of tourists wandered throughout while devoted Muslims bent forward in prayer, touching their foreheads to the carpet.

Muhammad Ali Mosque

Dan waited outside the mosque while Ali and I broke off in different directions. As I roamed on my own, I noticed a group of young veiled girls giggle and point at us. We were both used to getting stared at and it happened everywhere we went, but we must have looked pretty odd in our green cloaks because the girls couldn't seem to stop looking or laughing at us. When we were ready to leave, Ali and I found our flip-flops and the girls followed us outside. Two of them walked over and asked to take our photos. We all huddled together for several poses. The girls thanked us over and over and I couldn't help but feel we were now the best of friends.

Later, outside in the courtyard, I spotted a lone conservative Muslim woman dressed all in black from head to toe. I was instantly drawn to her and wanted a photo. Like a stalker, I followed her movements hoping to capture her dark and mysterious look, which seemed so exotic to me at the time. After moving stealthily around her and hiding behind walls, I took photo after photo. I was even able to take them without her noticing, and making a fuss. The photos turned out and are still among some of my favorites today. After living in Cairo for half a year and getting used to seeing more and more women covered completely in black, I finally got over my morbid curiosity.

On a Saturday afternoon trek on the edges of the city, Dan and I ventured into the City of the Dead, or *al-Arafa* (the cemetery). Located on the west side of the Nile, it's a four-mile long cemetery turned into a residential neighborhood where impoverished Egyptians live alongside the corpses. The expanse of Al-Arafa is surrounded by thick cement walls that separate it from the rest of the city. Young and old live in large windowless tombs that are built close together. Families convert the flat surfaces of the smaller tombs into tables and use the grave markers as shelves for laundry. Children play games of soccer and hide-and-seek between the abundant tombs, while funeral processions take place around them. Due to expensive rents and a shortage of housing in Cairo, many Egyptians have no choice but to make al-Arafa their permanent homes.

A large population of Egyptians inhabited the City of the Dead, but on that particular afternoon no one was around and the peacefulness felt eery. I caught a quick glimpse, however, of a small boy's round, vacant eyes as he peered out from a darkened doorway. The afternoon sun beat down on us as we wandered down one crooked path into another. I trailed behind Dan, who steered us through the confusing labyrinth of dirt paths trying to find a way out. He turned right, then left, and each path we took resembled the one before. A little less than an hour later, after several more turns, we reached the exit and strode out of al-Arafa. It took us nearly an hour to get through the desolate cemetery and I was more than relieved to enter the living and breathing of Cairo again.

The bearded taxi driver weaved his way through heavy traffic driving at breakneck speeds. I groped in the backseat for the seatbelt and finding none, grabbed onto the handle above the window and hung on. Dan gripped the dashboard as he attempted to tell the driver to slow down, but he either didn't understand English, or just pretended not to hear him. When the taxi ride from hell finally ended, Ali and I jumped out the minute the driver hit the brakes. Dan paid him the fare and shaking his head, slammed the car door.

"Do you believe he was mad because I didn't give him more money? Dan asked. "He drove like a maniac and is just lucky we didn't get into an accident."

Shaken from the hectic ride, we got off near the red brick Egyptian Museum of Antiquities in downtown Cairo. On the way there the taxi driver sped past the American University of Cairo campus and Tahrir Square, both popular tourist sites. A bit rundown and cluttered, the museum is home to King Tut and 120,000 other rare Egyptian artifacts and treasures. Two giant-sized stone pharaohs sit near the entrance to the museum on immense thrones, greeting visitors as they enter. The museum seemed so large and there were so many objects to look at, I knew I would never be able to see it all.

We chose to view only the best exhibits and among them, the solid gold burial mask of King

Tutankhamen, located in the basement of the museum along with other artifacts from his tomb. I skipped the Animal Mummies, but did go inside the Royal Mummy Room. Ramses II, the longest reigning pharaoh of ancient Egypt, lay in the room with dry strands of his original hair and his yellowed toenails still intact.

All of the antiquities and artifacts were very well-preserved in the museum and cared for with great patience, however, in 2015, King Tut's beard broke and when museum curators put it back together they used the wrong glue. After owning up to their mistake, they were relegated to other jobs in the museum.

Ian, Ali, and friend, in front of Egyptian Museum

By the end of three months I thought we'd hit all the major tourist attractions within Cairo. Garbage City, also known as *Manshiyat Nasser*, didn't sound like a must see, but Dan insisted we check it out anyway. On the day of our trip, we stood waiting longer than usual to be picked up. Several taxis stopped, but when we told them where we wanted to go they just shook their heads and sped off. It seemed that Cairene taxi drivers didn't like driving to this poor area, located at the base of the Mokattam Hills.

When the long awaited ride finally arrived and the driver agreed to take us to our destination, the three of us jumped inside. While we lurched along the winding streets amidst numerous traffic jams I could tell from the rancid smell of garbage lurking in the air that it was close by.

Garbage City is a slum inhabited by the Coptic Christians, called *Zabaleen* (garbage people) of Cairo. The mostly Christian families lived amidst the city's garbage, collecting, sorting, recycling, and selling what was left behind by Cairo's citizens. Driving haltingly along the narrow streets, our driver asked if we wanted to stop. Hemming and hawing, I told him that we could see just fine from the inside of the taxi. Our driver followed pickup trucks swaying back and forth with overloaded bundles of trash and we drove past donkeys straining to pull their overflowing wooden carts. Giant sacks of rubbish clogged the few available open spaces along the muddy streets, and our driver narrowly missed running into one or two of them. From our seats we watched shoeless children and adults in ratty clothes work side by side on the very tops of putrid piles of refuse. As a mother I was distressed to see so many children performing the same backbreaking work as the adults. I doubted any of them went to school, since their families needed them to work. Cairo had so much garbage I truly believed the residents of Garbage City were doing an important service. Without the waste management system they provided for the city, Cairo citizens would surely end up buried under the ever-present rubbish.

Also located in the area was the Cave Church of St. Simon, the largest church in the Middle East. In 1969 the Egyptian government forced all Coptic Christians to move to the outskirts of Cairo where they built churches inside the caves of Mokkattam. This time we got out of the taxi to get a closer look. Ali and I were rendered speechless at the impressive engravings, carvings, and mosaics that filled the massive walls of the caverns. The architecture of the church was like nothing I'd ever seen before and it was truly inspiring to witness what the shunned Christians had built for themselves. Garbage City and the Cave Church turned out to be one of the best sites in all of Egypt.

10

HOT AND COLD

After enduring three months of blistering hot temperatures, my body got used to Cairo's hot, dry climate. Then November, and winter in the desert hit, and the temperatures dropped forty degrees. Surprised that it could get so windy and bitterly cold in the desert, I was thankful I brought warm sweaters and jackets in my luggage. During the hot, dry days of the summer months when it became so unbearable that we craved cooler temperatures, I never believed the teachers when they said the weather would get cold.

"We're from Wisconsin," I always said, "we're used to some pretty harsh weather. Nothing will faze us!"

That November and December, my body went into shock from the biting cold temperatures that suddenly hit Cairo. The skies were overcast and the days bleak with little or no sun. When there was sun, it never stayed out long enough to warm me up. Daytime temperatures hovered around 40 degrees (Fahrenheit) feeling cold enough for snow in the desert. However, life around Cairo pretty much stayed the same--trees kept their leaves and stayed green and shopkeepers kept their doors open. Some Cairenes, however, did wear woolen hats and wrapped warm scarves around their necks during the coldest weather.

I tried desperately to keep warm in the teeth-chattering cold that seemed to creep beneath my clothes and into my bones, no matter how many layers I wore. The aching cold spread throughout my body like a virus and I had to blow onto my fingers and rub my arms often to warm myself. The school, with its cement and marble floors and walls, radiated cold making it even chillier than outside. There were no heaters in any of the classrooms or offices, leaving the school constantly frigid and drafty. Each morning before school, I piled on two or three layers of warm clothing. First, I yanked up my tights, then tugged on leggings over the tights, and over that, I pulled on my pants and struggled to button them closed. A sweater, coat, wool scarf, knit hat, and gloves completed my ensemble, which I even wore inside the school building. For once I envied the Muslim women with their arms, legs, and necks completely covered. They were not at all bothered by the ice-cold temperatures. Their usual attire of long and heavy garments was suffocating in the hot weather, but perfect for the months of bitter cold.

Dan suffered from the cold weather because he hadn't bothered to pack any warm clothing. He shivered throughout the bleak days and finally broke down and bought a warm jacket on a weekend shopping trip to Carrefour, Cairo's version of Wal-Mart. Inside the store, lanes filled with packaged foods stood adjacent to aisles holding racks of men's and women's clothing. Dan found some outdated corduroy blazers hanging near the cereal aisle and bought three in different colors. He wore one to school the next day and was surprised by all the compliments he got from his high school students. Never a fan of winter weather, I was miserable during those cold months. Who would have ever thought the desert could be so cold!

✹

The second semester of school was long without any breaks. We looked forward to the week-long spring vacation in March and planned another trip into the desert. It was to be Ali's final trip with us before graduating high school in June, and leaving Cairo for good. Overjoyed to leave the noisy and crowded city behind, we headed to the Black and White Deserts of the *Bahariya* Oasis, a five hour trip from Cairo. I was never a fan of camping, but Dan and Ali were excited to spend a night in the desert and again, I went along with it. At least the desert was flat, I thought, and I wouldn't have to climb any more mountains.

Dan rented a van and driver to take us to the town of *Farafra*, in western Egypt. Once there we stopped at a hotel and met up with Mahmoud who we arranged to take us on an overnight trip into the middle of the desert. After he and Dan chatted awhile, Mahmoud took us to his rattletrap 4x4 Jeep. He organized all of the camping gear and loaded the back with tents, sleeping bags, food, water, and everything else we needed for our campout.

Ali and I waited in the dusty parking lot while Dan and Mahmoud checked to make sure everything was packed. When all was in order, we climbed into the Jeep and set off. For the first fifteen minutes, Mahmoud drove over a smooth, flat main road, but soon turned off the highway onto a wide open space filled with rutted paths and numerous sand dunes. I clung tightly to the door handle as Mahmoud pressed harder on the gas pedal. From the backseat, Ali and I were tossed around like popcorn in a popper. The ride ended forty-five minutes later and I crawled out the door onto the blackened sand, feeling battered and bruised. The landscape surrounding us was desolate and barren. Mahmoud explained to us how the Black Desert got its name from the mountains that eroded and coated the area with blackish rocks and powder. Small volcano-shaped hills surrounded us and Dan ran to the tallest one, attempting to climb it. I rolled my eyes as he slipped and fell on his back numerous times, much like a child.

After trekking across a small area of the Black Desert we made our way over to the Jeep. Mahmoud drove us south across more rugged terrain until we got to the White Desert, an area with such unusual chalk-covered rock formations that it looked like another planet. We stared out the Jeep windows hardly believing our eyes. Strange mushroom-shaped boulders and sculpted grayish-white rocks jutted out of the ground in all directions.

Mahmoud drove us further into the desert along wide, frequently used paths created by the many Jeeps and SUV's that came before us. He stopped behind one of the colossal rock sculptures and proclaimed it to be a perfect spot for our campsite. I opened the door, jumped down onto the white sand and took a few steps toward the bizarre structures. I couldn't help but exclaim over the weird-looking place we were in and set off to explore. I took photos of the massive boulders trying to capture their strangeness. It was hard to believe the entire area was once underwater and a part of the sea. Throughout the area, seashells and whale bones could still be found beneath the sand.

While the three of us walked around in different directions taking in the craggy geological formations, Mahmoud started setting up the tents and firing up his mini-grill. In short time he had erected a place for us to sleep and cooked us a tasty dinner of grilled chicken and rice. He laid a camel blanket across the sand and we ate our simple meal under a black sky lit up with a billion pinpricks of bright stars.

Before I climbed into the tent for the night, I wandered off to take a bathroom break. With no toilet facilities anywhere in the desert, I went in search of a boulder to crouch behind. Peeing out in the open with no toilet paper, or sink to wash my hands, is one of the many reasons why I loathe camping. I tried hard to be a trooper, though, and contained my whining until we were back in the van headed for home. After I relieved myself, I made my way back to the tent. With the flashlight beaming ahead of me, I walked through the darkness hoping and praying I wouldn't step on any scary desert animals. Before I crawled into my sleeping bag, I brushed the sand off my clothes and took off my dusty Nike sandals leaving them outside the tent. I hated having sand stuck to me and knew I would never sleep if it was located on my body or inside my sleeping bag (the other reason I loathe camping).

It was our first time camping in the desert and we trusted Mahmoud to protect us. I did wonder, however, what kind of nocturnal animals or insects might prowl around our tent, but not long after I crawled into my sleeping bag I fell into a sound, dreamless sleep. The next morning I woke up groggy and stiff from sleeping on the hard ground. Desperate to get out and pee again, I groped outside the tent flaps for my sandals. I picked up what was left of them. During the night, a nocturnal animal had turned my Nikes into a tasty snack, chewing them to bits.

Still having to pee, I hunted in my bag for my flip flops. I found a pair and dragged myself out of the tent, getting as far away as I could. I scoped out a couple of areas, but when I walked into the bright morning sunlight I found that other campers had already used the best spots for their own personal toilets. In fact, each time I found a good-sized boulder to stand behind, another camper had beaten me to it. It wasn't evident during the dark desert night, but in the stark morning sunshine human feces everywhere, turning the desert into a huge outdoor toilet.

The White Desert was quite a spectacular site with its unusual and surreal beauty. I still consider it to be one of the most unique places I've ever been to.

Ali sitting on a rock sculpture in the White Desert

Upon our return to Cairo, we learned it was nearing time for the Hajj, the annual pilgrimage to Mecca in Saudi Arabia. Mecca was listed as one of the five pillars of Islam and Muslims were encouraged to make the trip at least once in their lifetime. Thousands of young and old devotees gathered together wearing their simple white garments, meant to portray that all Muslims were created equal in the eyes of God. Members of our teaching staff also attended and were given time off from school.

The *Eid-Al-Adha* holiday was celebrated at the end of Hajj. During this four-day festival, sheep and other animals were slaughtered for the Eid meal. Families purchased a sacrificial sheep, tied its legs together, and transported it live in the backs of pickups and in the trunks of taxis. From our apartment we heard the sad, mournful bleating of the sheep as they stood outside on balconies awaiting their fate.

11

SAVE THE ANIMALS

Whether camels, sheep, donkeys, or dogs, it was difficult for me to get used to the inhumane way that animals were often treated in Egypt. I witnessed dogs and camels being kicked and whipped, and donkeys forced to carry burdens at least twice their size.

Inside our apartment on a weekday afternoon, the unmistakable cries and yelps of a street dog brought me running to my living room window. I looked down at the street below and saw three teenaged boys viciously pelt a small, skinny dog with rocks. Horrified at their cruelty, I swung the window wide open and screamed out to them, "STOP! STOP IT." They ignored my pleas while continuing to chase the dog.

Emaciated dogs roamed the streets of Cairo alone and in packs. Fearful of abuse, the dogs slunk along with their tails between their legs scrounging for food scraps wherever they could find them. Many Muslims considered dogs unclean and I heard outrageous stories of street dogs beaten to death. It was heartbreaking to see innocent animals treated that way.

A stray white dog with matted and grimy fur began slinking around us in the early mornings as we waited for the school van. The poor animal was skin and bones and had several bald patches in his fur. I felt sorry for her and started bringing food each morning. Soon after, however, we left Cairo for the Christmas break and when we returned we looked for her. Sadly, we never saw the dog again, and assumed with no one around to feed her she moved on, or worse, died.

Donkeys, I believe, also had hard lives in Egypt. Used as beasts of burden, they were whipped and forced to pull heavy wagons or carry huge loads on their backs. Coming home on the school van one day, I looked out the window and noticed a small gray donkey struggle to pull a hefty wooden cart uphill. While the tired animal pulled and strained, I watched as it suddenly collapsed and fell to the ground. The farmer whipped it over and over, forcing it to stand, but it never moved. I could barely watch the scene from my window and wanted to scream at the van driver to stop so I could jump out and put an end to the farmer's beatings. I stayed put, though, and the van drove on. All night I thought about that poor donkey and wished I had done something. Still overcome with grief the next day, I watched from the van window as we drove past the area again. I scoured the path to see if the donkey was there, but it wasn't and I only hoped it had somehow survived.

The cruelty I witnessed toward animals will forever tarnish my feelings and memories of my time in Cairo.

On the other hand, Egyptians adored cats. Felines had glamorous histories that dated all the way back to the time of the pharaohs, when they believed that cats had special powers. A story exists about the prophet Muhammad who once found a cat sleeping on his robe and rather than disturb its peacefulness, simply cut a big hole around it. The Arabic word for cat is *Mau,* and it's also the name of the special breed that bears a distinct "M" mark on its forehead. Two dark lines also run from a Mau's eyes to its cheeks, and the heavy black eye makeup worn by ancient Egyptian women is believed to have been copied from the Maus. Also known for their piercing green eyes, spotted coats, and friendly natures, Maus today are much sought after around the world and people adopt them for their exotic looks and their intelligence.

Egyptian Mau Clubs and rescue missions held fundraisers in support of the cats. We attended one of the fundraisers where photos of adoptable cats were displayed while alcohol flowed freely among the guests. Later in the night after several drinks, a group of us performed a skit where we mewed and scratched like Maus in heat. We called ourselves "Dan and the Pussycats."

I am not a cat person and the large number of strays that prowled the streets repulsed me. They were everywhere hissing, skulking, and mating. I got up one morning and looked out my living room immediately spotting two large cats humping away. To be fair, the cats did aid in catching mice and rats, which I hated even more, and only once did we find one in our apartment.

Nearly asleep in my bed, Dan came upon a mouse and woke me up to help him catch it. I ran into the kitchen where he had it cornered. While he shifted some furniture to make a getaway path, I grabbed a broom to try to force the mouse to exit our apartment. Squeamish about the mouse running across my feet, I put on a pair of Dan's size twelve sneakers that sat nearby, praying the thing wouldn't crawl into the huge opening between the top of the shoe and my foot. I got into position, bent my knees, and crouched down like I was about to block a soccer goal. Dan admonished me to stay still while I held my breath waiting for the ugly, gray rodent to show itself. When I saw the hairy thing scurry toward the exit, I blocked it with my broom and let out a scream. The mouse ran out of the kitchen straight into the hallway and Dan slammed the door on it. We high-fived and went off to bed content that we were now mouse-free.

A sad and overworked donkey

12

DAILY LIFE

The summer break from school was two months long, but it never felt long enough, especially since it took an entire day to fly across the world and get back to our home in the U.S. The flights were long and boring, and we always arrived in Wisconsin drugged with jetlag. Our two months at home was spent relaxing and enjoying the clean Wisconsin air, green fields of lush grass, and woods filled with wild flowers, so different from the dry desert of Egypt. We also spent time with Ian and enjoyed get-togethers with friends and relatives. Dan and I caught up on all the news we missed during the months we were away and I binge-watched the latest movies and hit the shopping malls in my hometown.

Then, before we knew it, summer vacation was over and we were on the plane headed back to Egypt. In July, Dan and I flew to Cairo for our second year. Our contract was for two years and we would have to decide by the end of the year if we wanted to renew.

Ali had completed her senior year in Cairo at the end of our first year. She spent three weeks in Europe, then returned to Wisconsin and stayed to attend college. She was happy to be back with her friends and looked forward to being on her own. Living and going to school in Cairo, Egypt, was now relegated to the back of her mind, along with all of her memories of living overseas.

On our own this time, we started our second year in a different apartment in Maadi. We never liked the location of the first apartment, across from a bar and restaurant that was always noisy and crowded. Also, the longer we lived there the more rundown it felt and the lack of windows made it feel as though we were living in a cement box.

We found another apartment on the second floor in a building that was in a better location. After our return from the summer vacation, we packed everything into boxes. Dan went out into the street and coerced a couple guys with a truck to help us move. Willing to assist us for a few Egyptian pounds, the men filled the back of their small Toyota pickup with our belongings and Dan led the way to the apartment. After everything was unloaded, he paid the guys and walked back to get me.

"I can't believe it," he announced when he walked in. "The place is a pigsty. She left garbage all over the tables and floor. I need to bring garbage bags to clean up so that we can move in!"

It was frustrating to hear that the previous tenant left the place a mess, especially as she was one of the expat teachers at our school, and we knew her well. We spent the day cleaning and happily moved our things in once we had finished. The new apartment had more light and space and we felt safer being on a higher floor. The main door into the apartment opened up onto the living room, with its floor to ceiling windows. The dining room was up a step from the living room and a long table with six chairs filled the space. There was a small kitchen with little counter space and one small sink, making it difficult to wash dishes without getting water all over the floor. Our one large bedroom had a small closet where I kept my clothes, but Dan had to make do and hang his clothing on a makeshift pole that hung in the hallway between the living room and bedroom. The one feature that made the apartment somewhat charming was the small balcony located off of our bedroom. Even though there was only room for two people, I still enjoyed relaxing out there and watching the hustle and bustle of the street below.

The apartment building was located on Road 244, above a shoe store. Stores, hair salons, bakeries, and restaurants lined the road and we walked easily from one shop to another. There was always a lot of activity and I felt more in touch with local Cairenes as I lived and shopped alongside them. Some of the shops had unusual names, such as "What Women Wants" and "Walk like an Italian," which made me chuckle every time I walked past.

We met the bawab, Abu, soon after moving into the building. He spoke no English, but was always friendly and willing to carry our luggage or receive grocery deliveries for us. Abu lived with his wife and three small children in a tiny room on the first floor across from an ancient elevator that clanged loudly when it moved up and down. Each day after arriving home from school, I walked past their room with the door slightly ajar. Peeking in, I spied only two pieces of furniture: a queen-size bed that took up the entire room and a flickering television that played at full volume. Abu's wife and children perched on the bed and peeked out at me as I walked past to climb the stairs. Dan liked to bring the kids small toys or sweets and they always gave him a big smile in return.

Dan hired a maid to clean our apartment once a week. Noor always came during the hours we were at school and we never saw her much, but every Wednesday we arrived home to find our dishes washed, our clothes ironed, and the apartment spotless. It worked out perfectly since Noor only spoke Arabic and we would have had a hard time communicating with her anyway.

Road 244 was always at its quietest in the early morning. A few scraggly dogs roamed around and a couple of taxis idled nearby, but for the most part the busy streets were silent. Street sweepers were also out sweeping up the vast amount of garbage that littered the roads. It was always the same ancient woman who wore castoff rags and carried a large broom that swept our street each morning. She pushed the garbage from one side to the other, but never actually got rid of it. Dan gave her a few coins anyway, and she always thanked him with her big, old toothless smile.

Dan liked doing the weekly food shopping and got to know the shop vendors who called him the "big American." He bought our fruits and vegetables from outdoor stalls and couldn't get enough of the local honey-filled pastries available at the neighborhood bakery. Dan's biggest thrill though, was getting his weekly haircut. He didn't mind who cut his hair and he always got the same buzz cut. However, it was the soothing head and neck massages he got from the Egyptian barbers that kept him going back for more.

For me, getting a haircut was a nightmare, especially in a new country. It seemed that most women around the world had long, straight hair, and it was the same in Cairo. My hair on the other hand, was short, wavy, and unmanageable and I always feared having it cut. On a Saturday morning when I couldn't stand my unruly mane one minute longer, I left the apartment in search of a hair salon. I decided to go to the one nearest our apartment and walked the two blocks to Nefertiti's Hair Salon. I liked the fact that it was named after Egypt's most beautiful queen, and went inside. I was instantly greeted by a young man who of course, spoke no English. He showed me to a chair where I attempted to mime a scissors cutting my hair. With more hand gestures I showed him just where I wanted him to cut. While he nodded his head vigorously, I relaxed, wanting to believe he understood.

Taking a deep breath, I let him go at me. Thirty minutes later he finished and looked very pleased with the outcome. Not wanting to hurt his feelings I nodded and smiled, and paid for my cut giving him a generous baksheesh. Without even a glance in the mirror, I said goodbye and dashed out the door. Race-walking back to our apartment, I seriously hoped I would get back before I saw anyone I knew. I rushed inside, slammed the front door, and ran straight to the bathroom mirror where my reflection stared back at me. I grabbed a hand mirror to check out the back of my head and with an anguished groan realized he gave me a mullet. I tried fixing it, even cutting more off, but there was nothing to be done. I just had to wait for my hair to grow out, and I vowed never to return to Nefertiti's Hair Salon.

✳

Dining out in Cairo is also a popular pastime for tourists and Egyptians. There were many international and Egyptian restaurants to choose from, but none served alcohol. A well-loved feature of most of them was their willingness to deliver food right to your door. Chicken, burgers, pizza, kafta, shawarmas, and whatever else you desired would be delivered in thirty minutes or less by an Egyptian man on a motor scooter. Along with Cairo's restaurants, there was also American fast food, and it was the first time I lived in a city where I could have McDonald's Big Macs and french fries delivered to my door. Alcohol and pork products were available if you looked hard enough and knew where to find them. The expat teachers were often able to find the forbidden items, and even had them delivered.

A welcoming plate of hummus and ketchup

Italian food was always my favorite and one of the best restaurants was located in our neighborhood just a five-minute walk from our apartment. It was modern and spacious, and had a curved stairwell that led up to its second floor. Both floors had small seating areas that included soft, comfy couches and glass coffee tables. The menu was filled with a variety of Italian dishes, but the highlight for me was the heavenly chocolate lava cake that oozed a plate-sized puddle of delicious dark chocolate sauce. Who knew that Egyptians could do chocolate so well?

Eating out or buying food in countries with hot climates can be a real issue. In countries where the power goes off frequently and there is little or no refrigeration, foods become spoiled very quickly. Some of the countries don't have the same health standards as the U.S. and often disregard expiration dates. Spoiled foods are not always taken off the shelves and the unaware shoppers who purchase them end up with food poisoning. Thankfully, I never had it, but Dan did get sick while in Cairo. He became violently ill after eating a hamburger he bought at a neighborhood restaurant. Needless to say, he never ate hamburgers again in Cairo.

Egyptian men were big cigarette smokers. The teachers at our school even had their own smoking area right outside the gate where they met daily to get in a few puffs between classes. They also loved their sweetened tea and the men often congregated in the *ahawy balady* (coffee shops) where they drank tea, smoked cigarettes, and puffed on *hookahs*. Smoking hookahs, or shisha pipes, was also a popular pastime and restaurants and coffee shops supplied them for patrons of all genders. Waiters ran from table to table, filling the hookahs with water and fruit flavored tobacco. Customers inhaled deeply on the long snake-like tubes, forcing the water inside to bubble. Thick smoke hung in the air permeating everything in the restaurant with the sickening sweet smell of apple, lemon, and orange flavored tobacco. The potent odor of the tobacco was so overpowering that I often left the restaurants feeling nauseous.

I looked forward to my weekends when I could shop in Maadi. I loved to browse the many tourist shops that sold arts and crafts, antiques, silver jewelry, and colorful textiles. The intricate and colorful Bedouin embroidery adorned with tiny cross stitches, and the unique embellished bags, shawls, scarves, pillows, and clothing hand sewn by Bedouin women were like narcotics to me. I had to have more and more. I purchased so many of the one-of-a-kind creations brought to Cairo from remote areas of the Sinai that our apartment started to resemble a traditional Bedouin camp.

My favorite vendor, Omar, often sat on the steps of his shop reading the newspaper and watching people pass by. Whenever I was near, he waved and invited me in to see his latest acquisitions. Before I left Cairo, I made one final trip to say goodbye to Omar and since it was my last trip to his shop I couldn't leave empty handed. I left with a set of Egyptian cotton sheets, a hand woven Egyptian rug, and an antique Bedouin niqab.

I first got hooked (no pun intended) on hand woven rugs and carpets while living in Singapore where Dan and I attended carpet auctions at major hotels. Always on the lookout for more, I eventually located the one and only carpet shop in Maadi. Each time I walked by I gazed in rapture at the piled high stacks of wool, cotton, and silk Persian and Egyptian rugs. On one of our weekend walks through the neighborhood, Dan surprised me by walking up to the shop. He thought it would be a good idea to purchase a prayer rug, and wanted one in our home so that our Muslim guests could use it to pray. I followed him inside and upon entering, the salesman and his helper stood up and started taking down rug after rug for us to look at.

Overwhelmed by the choices, and after an hour of going through the stacks, Dan decided on one he liked. He chose a navy blue wool rug with an intricate floral border, and paid for it. The salesman's helper rolled it up, threw it over his shoulder, and carried it the five blocks to our apartment. Dan found a place for it on the living room floor where it wouldn't get walked on. Prayer rugs have symbolic meanings and meant to be taken care of in a holy manner. After months of having no Muslim guests however, the carpet eventually got stepped on, and even worse, Dan left his dirty sneakers on it. Our special prayer rug now covers the floor of our son's bedroom back home in Wisconsin.

Egyptian girls weaving rugs

I made it my mission to learn which shops in Maadi had the best merchandise and the best prices, and which of the vendors were willing to haggle. One of the best roads for shopping and dining was Road

9, a tourist street that included a Baskin Robbins, coffee shops, and a used bookstore that sold English books. It also had a variety of restaurants and cafes, along with shops that sold ornate, lattice-patterned *mashrabiya* furniture, carved marble knick-knacks, and silver cartouche pendants with Egyptian hieroglyphics.

One weekend, after a scrumptious pancake breakfast at Lucille's, a popular expat restaurant, Dan and I walked the entire length of Road 9. We drifted past the large McDonald's on the corner and set off in the direction of our apartment. We strolled along the sidewalks, moving onto the road whenever one abruptly ended, or was too torn up to walk on. When we attempted to cross the road, a frail, wretched-looking woman with two young girls trailing behind her approached us with her hands held out. The woman mumbled something in Arabic and pointed her crooked finger toward the girls' shoeless feet. Dan and I glanced at their grimy, dirt caked toes and I instantly felt distressed. I told Dan that she must need money to buy shoes for her daughters.

Instead of giving her money right away, and to make sure she actually bought shoes, we walked along with her to a nearby shoe store. We followed her in and she shuffled straight toward the one and only rack full of girls' shoes, almost as if she knew it was there. The woman pointed to a small black pair and the sales clerk picked them up and handed them over to Dan. The two little girls sidled up to him and gazed longingly at the shiny, black shoes. Dan took out his wallet and as soon as he paid the sales clerk the greedy woman grabbed the shoes out of his hands. Without so much as a thank you, or a smile, she left the shop with both girls in tow.

Fifteen minutes later, directly across the street, I spotted the three of them again. The woman had her hands out begging while the girls followed behind, still shoeless. I stopped and leered at her.

"Look. There she is and she's pointing to the girls' feet. Were we just scammed by that woman?" I asked incredulously.

"I think so!" Dan exclaimed. "I bet she's even in cahoots with the shoe shop!"

We saw the three of them many more times pacing up and down Road 9 looking for unsuspecting tourists. I never once saw the girls with shoes on their feet and it dawned on me that this was probably how the poor woman survived; she was a professional scammer who used the shoeless girls to take money from tourists. It was rather ingenious.

13

PHARAONIC FATIGUE

As our time in Cairo started to come to an end I began thinking about the places and things I still wanted to see and do. I knew once I left Cairo I would not get back anytime soon and I didn't want to have any regrets. So that's how I came up with the idea to get tattooed in Cairo. Tattooing was becoming more popular and there were now places where it could be done and people no longer had to leave the country. I also liked that it was much cheaper than in the U.S. I wasn't interested in getting a butterfly or a heart, but instead wanted to try cosmetic tattooing, specifically on my lips. I found Irma's name on a bulletin board; she advertised herself as a tattoo artist and I called her for an appointment.

Irma arrived at my apartment on a weekend in mid-May. A small, thin woman who spoke with a heavy Russian accent, she introduced herself at the door and entered ready to get down to business. I showed her to the living room and she pulled out her tattooing gear from a large bag and asked for an electrical outlet. I located one near the couch, and she ordered me to lie down. I did as I was told and explained to her that I wanted my lips tattooed with a permanent color. As a self-proclaimed lipstick addict, I never go anywhere without gloss on my lips and I could only imagine how great it would be to have color on them again, like I did when I was young. Irma had me pick out a flattering pink shade and I made myself relax, while I dreamed about the gorgeous lips I would soon have.

It never occurred to me that so much pain would be involved. Irma came at me with an electric needle that buzzed like a dentist's drill and, I suddenly wondered if I should have put more thought into getting tattooed. In her quaint Russian accent, Irma admonished me to keep my head still, however, when that needle hit my lips with what felt like a thousand needle pricks pelting me at the same time, it was all I could do not to push her and her painful tattooing instrument against the wall. She finally pulled away after my whimpers got louder and more frequent and the tears flowed from my eyes at an alarming rate. It was more painful than giving birth, and it felt almost as long. I barely survived the first round and wasn't too thrilled when Irma explained I would need to have two more sessions.

The next day I didn't see much color on my lips, but they did swell up. I dreaded seeing Irma for the second round, but knew that it had to be done if I wanted those luscious-looking lips. After the second session she informed me that my lips weren't taking the color, which occasionally happens. I was disappointed, especially when I realized I had endured all that pain for nothing. However, when Irma then offered me discounted rates for permanent eyebrow and eyeliner tattoos, I took her up on it, ready to suffer a little more for beauty. My eyebrows and eyeliner came out perfect and ten years later they still look dark.

✳

Living across the world from family and friends got lonely at times, and we missed many weddings, baby showers, and birthdays. We were excited when Dan's sister and brother-in-law told us they were interested in teaching overseas and Dan got them both jobs at our school. They moved to Cairo and placed their three kids in the school. It was a rough start at first--their children weren't readily accepted at school, money was tight, and their small apartment was too cramped. They made it work, though, and six years later they are still living in Cairo and working at the same school. Their oldest son graduated from the high school in 2013.

Toward the end of the second year, five members of my family braved the nineteen-hour flight to visit us. Dan and I played tour guides and took them to all the typical tourist attractions. We had a crew of seven and each time we went out we had to flag down two taxis. It was always a desperate attempt to make sure the taxis stayed together and we all ended up at the same place at the same time. We were lucky that no one ever got lost.

During one of our adventures to the Khan al-Khalili bazaar, we walked among the labyrinth of narrow paths trying hard to stay together. After leaving we found our way back out onto the busy streets where we walked by a small heap of tattered rags lying in the middle of the sidewalk. As I crossed the street and got a little closer, my eyes locked onto a pair of adult feet that stuck out at odd angles. As I observed closer, I noticed the feet were attached to the twisted body of an elderly woman who was concealed beneath the pile, not breathing. The wind shifted and we all moved away giving her a wide berth as the smell of her decaying flesh filled the air. Oblivious pedestrians rushed by without even a glance and I wondered if the old woman had been sick, or if she was hit by a car. I hoped someone would come soon to take her sad, lifeless body away. It was hard to know what to do in such a situation, but I assumed the workers who picked up dead bodies along the roads would eventually come to collect her.

✸

It was already the month of April and in June we planned to leave Cairo for good. Dan suggested that we take one final trip to the Red Sea and made reservations for all of us to fly to *Hurghada*, another popular tourist resort. He also planned a trip to the historical and ancient burial grounds of Luxor's Valley of the Kings. Luxor was once the capital of Egypt and is known as the "world's greatest open air museum." Carved into the hills are sixty tombs that contain pharaohs and their wives, children, and in some cases, family pets.

The flight to Luxor from Cairo took barely an hour and we arrived there late in the sun-drenched afternoon. Once we got to the hotel, Dan organized a van to pick us up at dawn the next morning. He had booked us on a hot air balloon and it was scheduled to take us on an early morning ride over the Nile and the ancient Valley of the Kings.

Giddy with excitement, the seven of us woke the next morning before daylight and hopped onto a van. After a twenty-minute ride, the driver dropped us off near a large open field where five brightly colored balloons lay spread out on the ground, flat as pancakes. The air was chilly and the sky cloudy as workers sat around waiting for instructions. Balloons were not allowed to go up if the wind speed and weather conditions were not perfect, so we waited with them. Other groups of tourists stood nearby and I bided my time by eavesdropping on their conversations. I heard discussions of previous trips that were cancelled at the last minute due to bad weather. I hoped it wouldn't happen to us, as this would be our one and only opportunity to take a balloon ride in Egypt.

My eyes never once left the deflated balloons or the workers who crouched near them. After chatting with one another for over an hour we still had no idea if we were going up, but we continued to hope. Finally, we noticed movement around the balloons and in a matter of minutes the workers stood up, sprinted toward the baskets, and began shouting at one another in Arabic.

"Is this it?" I asked Dan. "Are we going up?"

Our group stood up and sprinted right behind the workers. We lined up outside one of the balloons and one-by-one, were lifted up and over the tall sides of the basket. When all twelve of us were inside, the captains tipped the basket onto its side. We stared into the blue sky as we waited patiently for the balloon to fill with air. It was a tight squeeze and we were forced to lie very close to one another. My 70-year old mother was pressed so tightly against a potbellied man twice her size that I was afraid she would be smothered before we even lifted off the ground.

Suddenly the balloon captains shouted loudly to one another and our basket bumped and swayed, righted itself, then lifted off the ground. "We're going up!" I shouted and my pulse quickened. I grabbed onto the ropes to steady myself and in a burst of excitement clapped and cheered along with the other riders. We floated higher and higher into the cloudless sky and the quiet of the still air was broken only by the periodic *whoosh* of the billowing fire heating the air inside the balloon. No one uttered a word as we sailed majestically across the sky. I surveyed the view from inside the basket and could make out miniature-sized statues, temples, and ruins below. Floating lazily over Luxor, I savored the panoramic views of green farmland that lay adjacent to the sandy desert. After an hour of drifting along, Dan got brave and leaned his body out of the basket snapping photos and chronicling our first hot air balloon ride.

The ride over Egypt was an extraordinary experience and one I'll never forget. It was almost as though the pharaohs and gods watched over us to make it a perfect day. We had put all our faith and trust into the local Egyptians, too, believing they'd follow all safety procedures. I was thankful we had a safe ride but that wasn't always the case for others who had taken balloons up.

A month after our own balloon ride, I learned one had collided with a cell phone tower and crashed to the ground, injuring sixteen tourists. Then, in February, 2013, I learned that a balloon caught on fire while in the air and nineteen tourists plummeted a thousand feet to their death. It was later learned that the pilot and maintenance engineer failed to make the proper safety checks before lifting off.

When our balloon landed on solid ground again, our hotel minivan picked us up and dropped us off at the main entrance to the Valley of the Kings. Soon after purchasing our entry fee into the site we secured a knowledgeable Egyptian guide who led us to the different sites giving us long explanations about each one. I'm normally not a huge fan of history, but I would have missed out on a vast amount of information if we hadn't had our trusty guide showing us around. However, after being bombarded with so many facts and information, along with the harsh and unrelenting sun beating down on me, I was soon overcome with mind-numbing pharaonic fatigue.

Despite my tired feet, the relentless heat, and scores of tourists, our visit to the Valley of the Kings was incredible. It was also a photographer's dream and everyone snapped photos making it virtually impossible to get shots with just family members. Looking at my photos later, there always seemed to be a stranger or two lurking somewhere in them, making the photos just a little less special.

Many areas in the royal burial grounds were roped off to tourists as archaeologists were still digging and uncovering artifacts and tombs long buried in the sand. The stroll down the Avenue of the Sphinxes took us between two rows of cat-like bodies that were made of stone and adorned with human heads. We ducked inside the Temple of Luxor and passed a thin and angry looking man standing guard at the entrance. With a scowl on his face, he eyed us warily as we all trooped past. After peering into the dark and dusty tomb we moved toward the exit. When we got close to the guard he suddenly jumped out and accused my mother of sneaking photos with her camera. The foolish guard even tried taking her camera away, but my mother held on tight and shouted at him to back off. He spewed rapid Arabic at her and tried again to grab her camera. Our group hurried toward the exit where Dan shouted at him in English.

"There's a guy right behind us who has a camera! Why don't you take his?" Dan bellowed.

Dan and I at the Valley of the Kings

Our tour ended with no more hassles or aggressive Egyptian guards. Scorched from the blistering heat and mentally drained from pharaonic fatigue, we left Luxor the next morning and boarded the plane to Hurghada. After the scorching hot days of Luxor, a stay at a hotel on the crystal blue sea was just what we needed.

At the hotel, we chartered *The Red Lady,* for a day trip. With the sun high up in the sky, our group boarded the boat and cruised out to sea. The captain steered us to an ideal location and we all jumped in the water and swam around magnificent coral reefs. We snorkeled in water so clear it felt as though we were inside a giant aquarium full of amazing species of fish and colorful, intricate coral. Angelfish, lionfish, hawk fish, and stingray flitted near the purple, red, and yellow coral looking like an underwater forest of gently swaying trees. The clear water, shallow reefs, and expansive plant and animal life made for a perfect last vacation on the Red Sea.

Around lunchtime the captain and his amiable crew plied us with drinks and fed us all a gourmet seafood lunch. We cruised along the water and just before heading back to shore, the captain announced that a pod of dolphins was swimming nearby. He steered the boat toward them and we arrived just in time to see ten dolphins frolicking in the water. Dan immediately jumped in after them and for a few seconds made contact with the sleek wet tail of one, just before it dove underwater and out of sight. I surprised myself when I also jumped off the side of the boat and into the water. However, all my kicking and thrashing about didn't help me in catching up to any of the dolphins.

After our last lazy day on the Red Sea, we caught another short flight back to Cairo. My family members spent their final day shopping for Egyptian trinkets and trying to squeeze them into already full suitcases. Around midnight a van picked them up in front of our apartment and took them to the airport. Dan and I waved goodbye to them knowing that in only a few short weeks we would see them again in Wisconsin.

✸

Our contract with the school came to an end that June, 2009. Dan and I made the decision to leave Egypt rather than sign up for another year. We were anxious to move on and experience another school and culture, something overseas educators often do, and there was still so much of the world we hoped to see.

On the final day of school, the teachers and students were in high spirits and we all looked forward to a long summer vacation. Halfway home, I was presented with a hardcover children's book about Egypt called *Goodnight My Cairo*, written by Mandy Fessenden Brauer, a children's author who I had invited to the school a few months earlier. Each teacher had written a personal and heart felt goodbye message in the inside cover. I was touched by the gift and to this day count it as one of my most treasured Cairo souvenirs.

When the van pulled up in front of our apartment for the very last time, I followed Dan out onto the curb. I turned and waved as the doors closed and the driver pulled back onto the busy street. With a heavy heart I hollered goodbye to friends I had known and worked with daily for the past two years, and whom I knew I might never see again.

The van sped off into the street just as Dan called out, *"Yalla* (let's go)!" And without a backward glance, I sprinted up the stairs to our apartment ready to pack up the mementos and memories of our extraordinary Egyptian adventure.

14

AUTHOR'S NOTE: LESSONS I'VE LEARNED

At the end of our two years in Cairo, Dan and I got the itch to move again and our enthusiasm soon took over. The thrill of adventure and the excitement of the unknown kept us looking toward our next journey. The many challenges of relocating to a new country were quickly forgotten, as we concentrated on what lay ahead.

The years had sped by quickly and every day felt like a mini-adventure. Dan and I knew there were many more experiences ahead for us and the frequent moves, excessive amounts of baggage, and daily challenges of living in a new culture never deterred us. We still continue to embrace the lifestyle of international education today.

After the years in Egypt, I got used to the brazen stares and being the only foreigner in the neighborhood. I became bolder and more confident than I was when I first traveled overseas with two toddlers. I've continually learned that in order to survive in this unconventional lifestyle I must be open to whatever comes my way. The years in Egypt gave me many opportunities to broaden myself and my view of the world, experience the ways of other cultures, and become more globally-aware.

As a result, I have learned to live my life by the following tenets:

Be brave. Fear only holds us back from experiencing all we can in life. Push yourself to try new things. Climbing Mt. Sinai was way out of my comfort zone. I had always preferred to look at mountains from the distance and could never understand why someone would want to actually go up them. But I did it, and I made it to the top. Years later, Dan and I still tell the story of how we almost divorced on that biblical mountain.

Be less afraid of embarrassing yourself. Don't worry about what others think of you as you attempt to speak their language and end up mangling the pronunciations. At least you gave it a try.

Be adventurous and investigate your new surroundings. Explore the towns, villages, and countryside. There was much to see in Egypt and we would have missed out on a lot of ancient and notable sites if we hadn't gone out and searched for them on our own.

Don't judge. Be open-minded about the ways of other cultures. Ask questions and learn as much as you can; it will open you up to a wider world. While living in a Muslim society I learned to respect their beliefs and traditions, no matter how different they were from my own. I wasn't expected to wear a hijab, but I did acknowledge Muslim women's reasons for doing so.

Get out and meet the local people. You'll probably get stared at, children will point at you and giggle, and babies may even fear you and start to cry. People will be curious about you because you look different from them. I believe that most people in the world, no matter where they come from, are naturally friendly and helpful. There were many times Dan and I asked for help, and everyone, from the people on the street to taxi drivers and market vendors, went out of their way to help or give us advice.

Greetings are very important in many cultures. Learn to speak them in the local language so that you can greet your neighbors, workers, shopkeepers, and taxi drivers. They will respect you more after you give them a kind word and a smile. The first words I learned in Cairo were the Muslim greeting, Salaam Alaikum, and I always received a kind reply in return.

Be spontaneous. The best things in life happen by chance. Be open to it all--good and bad. Our impromptu trip to the Red Sea only days after we arrived in Cairo was one of the best trips and some of the best diving and snorkeling experiences I ever had.

Learn to take life in stride. Accept that this is the way life is and the way things are done here, right or wrong. You will eventually get used to the power shortages, horrendous drivers, and the smell of sewage from the open drains.

Be patient. Life oftentimes is slower in other countries. When the party is scheduled to begin at 8:00 p.m., but no one shows up until 10:00 p.m., just roll with it. Even though Dan and I tried to get used to doing things at a later time (eating and sleeping), we found we just couldn't kick our American ways and continued to eat alone at restaurants, sometimes hours before the local patrons arrived. (We did get the best tables, though).

Get used to doing without the American foods you thought you couldn't live without because chances are you won't find them in your adopted country. In Cairo, I shopped at small local markets instead of large grocery stores like I was used to in the U.S., where I could find everything I needed. The few western foods that were on the shelves were often so overpriced that we just went without. Dan and I stuck pretty much to the same foods and ate them over and over again, but on the upside, we got a large variety of fresh veggies and fruits all year long.

Cell phone service and internet can be spotty, and if you lose power for an hour, a day, or even a week, no amount of complaining or cussing will help. Just load up on batteries, flashlights, and candles beforehand so you are ready when the time comes. Then to kill time because the air conditioner's not working and it's much too hot to sit in your apartment, go for a walk and explore the neighborhood. You will be amazed at what you'll find that you didn't even know was out there.

Most importantly, keep a sense of humor and learn to laugh more. I learned to take things less seriously and to find humor in situations where others just shook their heads in frustration. A "such is life" attitude goes a long way in relieving the stress of finding a plumber to fix the toilet, or while you're sitting in a traffic jam waiting for a herd of goats to cross the road. Living in a country where life is sometimes backwards is not always enjoyable, but finding a sense of humor can help you relax while you're there. When things don't make any sense, just chalk them up to the many quirks of living overseas.

Lastly, whether you bring along a travel partner or go it alone, how you adapt to a new culture and country can make or break your time overseas. Temperament, character, disposition, and stress level all play a part in whether or not you are fit for life abroad. If you choose to bring a partner, he or she is the one who will share in your good and bad times, the one who will take care of you if you get sick, and the one you have to be able to trust for advice and to watch your back.

My time overseas is much more fun with my husband by my side. He shares in my laughter, he keeps me safe, and he doesn't complain too loudly when I want to shop. While in Cairo, Dan hunted the streets for a plumber and electrician when we needed one, even though he didn't speak a word of Arabic. He scrounged around our neighborhood looking for a pizza restaurant because he knew I couldn't live without it. And he always found a grocery store nearby to keep me plied with chocolate and Coca-Cola.

Our unconventional lifestyle of living and working around the world has provided us with many incredible experiences. Our numerous exploits and accomplishments have turned us into better educators, braver adventurers, and more caring and passionate citizens of the world. I could've never asked for a more supportive and understanding travel companion, and knowing that Dan was with me through it all made my experiences that much more fulfilling.

Layla

ACKNOWLEDGEMENTS

A big thank you goes to the following people for taking the time to read and comment on my manuscript and for giving much needed advice on turning my story into a book:

Gisela Flores, Nirmala Chennemsetty, Lucinda Clarke, Scott Spotson, Christine Michael, Jo Vraca, and Bozena Brzeczek Masters

Special thanks to my editor, Silvia Curry, for her expert suggestions and feedback

And to Ali Dobbe, for allowing me to use her photos

ALSO BY AUTHOR:

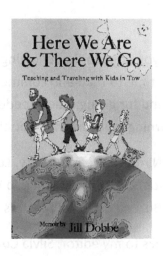

"Felt like I was there!"

"A fascinating tale of life overseas with children."

"Enjoyable! Couldn't put it down!"

"A thoroughly enjoyable travel read!"

"Delightfully entertaining!"

Facebook.com/jilldobbeauthor

Made in United States
Troutdale, OR
12/08/2024

26093895R00100